26 Weeks to Wealth and Financial Freedom

By

Debbi King

Copyright © 2013 by Debbi King

26 Weeks to Wealth and Financial Freedom
by Debbi King

Printed in the United States of America

ISBN 9781492326984

All rights reserved solely by the author. The author guarantees all contents are original and do not infringe upon the legal rights of any other person or work. No part of this book may be reproduced in any form without the permission of the author. The views expressed in this book are not necessarily those of the publisher.

Table of Contents

Introduction 7
Week 1 11
Week 2 23
Week 3 35
Week 4 43
Week 5 51
Week 6 59
Week 7 67
Week 8 75
Week 9 83
Week 10 93
Week 11 111
Week 12 119
Week 13 129
Week 14 141
Week 15 151
Week 16 161
Week 17 171
Week 18 181
Week 19 193
Week 20 201
Week 21 207
Week 22 215
Week 23 223
Week 24 231
Week 25 241
Week 26 249

INTRODUCTION

Have you ever wondered why some people seem to "have it all"? Do you find yourself wishing for "the good life"? Is financial stress something you deal with every day? Imagine having the answers to these questions, and the power to change the course of your life in only 26 weeks. This book will give you those answers and that power.

Wealth means different things to different people. To some, they would feel wealthy if they just had a couple of thousand in the bank. Many would feel wealthy if they were debt free. And to some, it is a magic number like one million dollars. Webster defines wealth as a great quantity of money, possessions and property. It does not define it by a certain dollar amount.

Wealth is not about a certain dollar amount. It is about a lifestyle and the result of that lifestyle being money. We all have the ability to be wealthy, so why are some people wealthy and others are not? It is not about luck and playing your cards right. It is about the steps you take and the decisions that you make on a daily basis.

Taken straight from the playbook of the wealthy, this book will teach you how to take those specific steps and make better decisions when it comes to your money. You will learn the secrets of the wealthy and what steps they took to get where they are. With the tools and skills you gather in just 26 weeks, you can live a life of wealth and financial freedom. Yes, you can be wealthy!

But it won't happen overnight. It won't happen using a magic wand or a magic pill. And there are no shortcuts. As you are going through this book, you will be tempted with two different shortcuts: one will be to read the whole book in one week and the other will be to skip a week or more thinking that you don't need it. But giving in to those shortcuts may hinder your wealth journey.

If you want to be wealthy and financially free, and obviously you do, you need to take what is in the book seriously. You need to focus on each week for a week and not skip anything. Everything in here is vitally important to your wealth journey. This book is not about getting rich quick or about making millions in just 26 weeks. This is a book about a lifestyle – the lifestyle of the wealthy. When you want to be something, you learn everything you can about that something so that you can be the best that you can be in that area. And being wealthy is no different.

I am going to go ahead and give away the ending. If you do everything that is in this book and keep doing it for the rest of your life, you will be wealthy and financially free. I can't tell you how long it will take because I don't know how bad your situation is, but it worked for me and I filed for bankruptcy over 15 years ago and literally started from scratch as a single mom and making $20,000 a year at the time.

You are an awesome person and you are stronger than you think you are. It doesn't matter what side of the tracks you were born on, where or if you went to college, or what you have done in the past. You can begin again and have the best life that you can possibly have. You can do this and this book will explain to you exactly how. I am so glad to be taking this journey with you and I can't wait to see how your life is going to change over the next 26 weeks. So without further ado, let's get started.

WEEK ONE

SET 3 YEAR GOALS IN ALL AREAS OF YOUR LIFE

Goal setting is a huge step in gaining success in anything. If you do not know where you are going, how will you know what you need to do to get there? Zig Ziglar always said that "a goal properly set is halfway reached." This means that just setting your goals and writing them down is half of the battle.

Two weeks of this program are dedicated to setting goals: first we address the "where do I want to be in 3 years" question and in a few weeks, we will delve into the short term and long term success goals that you have. The reason that we spend so much time in this area is because it is a foundation to a wealthy and successful life. If you don't have anything to aim for in life, you will just go through each day with very little purpose except to get up and go to bed. You need goals and dreams – something bigger and better to always be moving toward.

It is not enough to just have the goals and dreams in your head. A big key in achieving your goals is not only defining them, but also writing them down. You need to write out your goals in very specific terms as well as have a realistic plan and timeline for these goals.

For example, maybe one of your 3 year goals it to get out of debt – you can't simple say "I want to get out of debt in 3 years." You need to write down your goal and be specific. "I want to pay off my $33,253 in debt within 3 years." Then come up with a plan to do this. Simple math is you need to pay $923.69 per month toward this debt. But maybe your budget doesn't allow this much to be paid. So then, you have to decide how to come up with extra money in order to achieve your goal – do you need to do some extra work, do you need to sell something, or do you need to sacrifice in an area or two?

Goal setting needs 4 components in order to be successful. Goals need to be:

- ❖ Written
- ❖ Realistic
- ❖ Specific
- ❖ Adjustable

Written - You have to write your goals down so that you can see them every day and have a written plan for where you are heading. You would never take off on a trip across the country without a plan; otherwise, you would just be driving around for weeks or months and never get where you were going. You can't take off on the trip called "life" without a plan either.

Realistic - Your goals have to be realistic. If you set unrealistic goals, you will have trouble reaching them and the results will not be positive. In the example before, $ 33,253 in 3 years may not be realistic for you. Maybe you need 3 ½ years or 4, but be careful – make sure you aren't stretching your goal out because of procrastination. Don't set a goal to lose just ½ pound per week because you don't want to exercise. Remember, a goal is a plan for your dreams. Dream big, believe in the impossible, and be real.

Specific - Specific goals are the only goals that stand a chance of being met. When a goal is vague, it leaves too much room for interpretation and backing out. Being specific also helps you to focus. What you focus on is what you will achieve. If you say you want to lose weight, but never lay out how much and in what time frame, you will never lose weight and you might even gain weight out of a sense of failure. But if you set a specific goal of losing 1 pound per week, then you have a focus and you will put your time and energy into losing that pound every week.

Adjustable - And lastly, goals need to be adjustable. I don't mean that you need to change your mind every week and keep changing your goal. What I mean is that a goal needs some room for change as life happens, if necessary. Let's say you have a goal to go to the gym 3 times a week. Then all of the sudden you have a financial emergency and you have to give up your gym membership. This doesn't mean you have to give up your goal to exercise. If simply means you need to adjust your goal to fit your current financial situation. There are many ways to exercise for free.

Just this week, Diana Nyad swam from Cuba to Key West. She had dreamed of swimming this route for 35 years and finally, in her 5th attempt, she succeeded. In order to accomplish such a dream, she had to have goals that were written down, specific and realistic. And each time she did not succeed in meeting her goal of swimming the 110 miles, she had to adjust her goals and keep going. This remarkable woman had a dream for 35 years and never gave up on that dream. Every time she was knocked down, she got back up, dusted herself off, readjusted her plan with her new knowledge, and tried again. And at age 64, her dream came true. Even with her goals and plans, her trip wasn't easy. She had to deal with many elements in her 53 hour swim. But every time she thought of giving up, she said to herself "find a way. Find a way and you will make it through." This story should be inspiration to us all that with the right plans and goals and the right attitude, all of our dreams can come true.

WHERE DO I WANT TO BE IN 3 YEARS?

Now it is time for you to begin your life changing journey by setting 3 year goals in 7 very important areas of your life. You will want to make sure that every goal is written down, specific, realistic and adjustable. You want to make sure that you make goals in all 7 areas because you need to have balance in your life. For example, if you focus most of your time on your career, then you will end up neglecting your family, your marriage, and even your finances. Balance is key. So let's dive right in.

Career – Are you happy every day when you go to work or are you just going to a j-o-b for the m-o-n-e-y? Work is a very important part of our lives and a very necessary part, whether you are the CEO of a top Fortune 500 company or a stay at home mom. We work a minimum of 40 years of our lives – that is 83,200 hours out of our lives. 1/3 of your day is spent working – the same amount of time you spend sleeping. So it is vitally important that you enjoy what you do or you are just going to be miserable for a minimum of 1/3 of your life. When looking at where you want to be in your career in 3 years, I would encourage you to make sure your goal is set doing something you really enjoy. This may mean that you need to make a career change. Don't be afraid to do something new and exciting. Just make sure that your goals are in line with the other areas of your life. A great example would be if what you want to do requires that you go back to school for more education. Make sure that doing so doesn't interfere with your financial goals. There are many ways to get the knowledge and the experience you need to do what you love to do. Think outside the box and go for it. If we all worked in our calling and in our passion, this world would be a better place.

Family and Friends – For me, my family and friends are the most important people in my life. I have a very unique family situation which makes it even more special. I have noticed that over the years there have been many times where I have felt disconnected with my family and I feel like I lost some good years during that time. So for me, my family and friends goals must include staying in touch with each member, even my cousins, as much as I can even with something as simple as a birthday card or a thinking of you note. Maybe you are estranged from your family and your goal may be to reconnect with them. Maybe you are a little too close to your family and it takes away from your life and you need to set up boundary goals in order to keep your relationship positive. Whatever your situation is, we all need our family and friends – those relationships are important to our well-being and happiness. Maybe you need to make a goal to forgive someone who mistreats you; perhaps they don't even realize they do it. I had this happen to me in a very close relationship situation. Someone very dear to me would put me down and offend me almost every time I spoke with them. But I realized, it was just who they were. They weren't going to change so I did. I accepted them for who they are and made a goal to go out of my way to compliment them and praise them. You need to make sure that the goals you set in this area (and all of the others) move you in a positive direction. You can't change people, but you can change yourself and keep a positive attitude in every situation. Do what you can do and God will do the rest.

Marriage – Speaking of not being able to change people – this was the area of my life where this concept became the clearest. The goals that you set for your marriage need to be goals that will move your marriage in a positive direction. They should not be selfish goals like "I want to get my way more" or "I am going to point out my spouse's faults more". Your goals should lean toward actions that you can take to better your relationship and show your spouse the love and respect they deserve (even if they don't show it back). If you feel that your marriage is beyond hope, then maybe your goal needs to be to seek wise counsel to renew the relationship. The purpose of having goals and dreams is to move your life in a positive direction. This can be challenging in any area, but especially in the area of our marriages because we cannot control the other person. When you are making goals in the area of career or family or even money, you have control over whether you reach your goal or not. So make sure that the goals you set in the area of marriage are things that you can control, not goals to change the other person.

Personal Growth – Personal growth encompasses many different things, but is basically anything that will grow you and mature your thinking and help you gain knowledge. I use this area of goal setting as anything I can do to improve myself and grow into the person I want to be. Before setting these goals, take the opportunity to evaluate where you are in your life and who you are and then who and where you want to be. This can be hard because it means taking a good hard look at ourselves, and as was the case with me, sometimes that isn't too pretty. But don't be afraid to go there because there must be pain before there is gain. Some examples of goals in this area are:

- Reading non-fiction books – 1 per month
- Forming a new good habit to replace a bad habit
- Overcoming an addiction
- Taking a class just for fun to learn a new skill
- Limiting yourself with distractions such as television, email, computer games, Facebook, etc.
- Take on a new hobby

These are just a few examples – the world is wide open to you and the possibilities are endless. My hope for you is that your goals will lead you down a path of happiness and joy with a smile on your face, which is the ultimate goal.

Spiritual – This will mean different things for different people. I am a person of faith so for me it is about reading the Bible more and learning all I can about God so that I can have the ultimate close relationship with Him. But whatever you believe in, and we all believe in something, these goals should bring you into a place of peace and tranquility. We were not put on this earth to be stressed out and angry all the time. There is no point in that – it accomplishes nothing. So set your goals in the direction of meditation and taking time out for yourself every day. You need to find 30 minutes of peace every day. It may seem impossible, but it can change your life. Lock yourself in the bathroom if you have too, get up ½ hour earlier than everybody else, do whatever it takes to maintain peace and joy in your life.

Physical Health – I have found out the hard way just how important this area is. I have been overweight for many years of my life and I have missed out on so much. Then I got to the point where I had had enough. I realized I was worth more than this and I needed to stay around for awhile. I still struggle with my eating habits, mostly the kind of food that I eat, but I work at it all the time. I exercise 6 days a week – 3 days dancing my bum off to Latin music and having a blast. I decided to make a lifestyle change, not just go on a diet. And with the help of my family and an awesome personal trainer, I am healthier than I've been in a while. I am not where I want to be, but I am doing something about it. The goals in this area are not only about dieting and weight. They are also about some form of exercise. We all need to move and do some form of exercise at least 3 days a week. Set goals you can obtain and aim them toward a healthier you. You are awesome and we want you around for a long time to come.

Finances – Well, as you know, I could write a whole book in this area (and I have). But I will try to narrow it down for the purpose of goal setting. You want to make sure, just like in all of your goals, that you are not vague. You shouldn't simply say "I want to be out of debt" or "I want to be a millionaire". Even in this area, you need to be specific. In this area of goal setting, it is also very important to make sure that the goals are realistic. Many of us live champagne lives on beer budgets. You want to dream big and set life changing goals. In order to do this, you are also going to have to be very specific about what you are going to do to reach these goals – raise your income, lower your lifestyle, or a little of both. It is also important, if you are married or planning to be married in the next 3 years, that your financial goals include your spouse – their thoughts, their goals, their dreams and their ideas. You will be able to reach your goals quicker and much easier if you work as a team, which is what marriage is all about.

SUMMING UP WEEK 1

Here we are at the end of week one. I hope that you have learned something new about goal setting and that you can understand how important goal setting is. At this point, you should have set and written down at least one goal in each of the seven areas of your life. What I believe you will find, as I did, is that the further you get into the process, the more you will see how all of these areas work together to bring you to the life that you want for yourself in the next 3 years. In some cases you may find that you can't have one without the other – for example, you may not be able to reach your financial goals without your career goals. And that is what this week is all about. The first step to building wealth is laying out a plan – a balanced, realistic plan – and that is what you have accomplished this week. On to week 2!

WEEK 2

DEALING WITH YOUR DEBT

When wealthy people are interviewed for articles, for projects, or for books like "The Millionaire Next Door", you will never hear them say that debt is what made them millionaires. As a matter of fact, you will usually hear the opposite, that not having debt is one of the keys to their wealth. Having and using debt can be the biggest obstacle to you becoming wealthy.

To be able to get past this obstacle, you must first understand exactly what debt is and how to avoid having it in your life. Once you understand what debt is exactly then you can stop using debt going forward and remove the debt you have.

So, what is debt? Debt is not just credit cards, car loans or anything else with a payment plan and interest charge. There are wealthy people who use credit cards and who have car loans. Debt is when you owe more than you have – your liabilities are greater than your assets.

✳✳✳

When a wealthy person uses a credit card, they pay it off every month in order to avoid extra charges of any kind. They are using it as a convenience not a way of life. When a wealthy person uses a car loan to pay for the purchase of a vehicle, they have chosen to use the bank's money at 1.9% interest instead of losing 5% interest on the money they have in the bank. They will also put as much money down as they can and pay it off as quickly as they can.

✳✳✳

Simple math tells us that the only way to have money is to spend less than we make. Therefore, mathematically speaking, you can never be wealthy and have debt. Debt is money that you have reached into your future to use even though you haven't earned it or received it yet. This risk is what makes debt such a bad decision – the risk being that something could happen and cause you to not be able to earn or receive the money that you were betting on receiving. This kind of risk taking is the result of thinking like a broke person – thinking short term and small. To be a wealthy person, you must think like a wealthy person – long term and big. A wealthy person doesn't spend money that they do not have in their possession and they do not spend money that they may need in the future to live on or for an emergency.

If you want to be wealthy, and obviously you do or you wouldn't be reading this book, you must stop all debt going forward. When you are faced with a problem or a purchase going forward, your answer cannot include debt. This will become easier starting next week after you establish a budget and begin to tell your money where it needs to go. Right now, if you are not doing a budget, you are probably using debt such as credit cards in order to get through the month when you run out of money. Or you are using debt when emergencies arise and you panic due to a lack of cash. With a zero budget, you won't need to do that anymore. Having a budget will also help you to save and have money set aside for emergencies such as a car repair or home repair so that you will not need to use debt as an answer for your problems going forward.

✻✻

Many people chose to use loans against their 401K's at their jobs for emergencies or financial situations that may arise. The thought is that it is not debt because it is my money – "I am just borrowing my money at 5% interest which I am also paying back to myself." In that sense it is not debt, but there is a huge risk with this type of loan. When you leave your job (whether it is your decision or theirs), the loan balance at that time is considered an early withdrawal if it is not paid back immediately. This means you will owe a 10% penalty and a 30% tax to the IRS. So your 5% just became 40%. You may think you will never leave your job, but the average time at a job currently is 3.7 years. You must think long term and not take this risk.

✻✻

We are a society that has accepted debt as a part of life. Many people believe that debt is just a part of life and normal. Do you know what else the new normal in our society is? Being broke and living paycheck to paycheck. But this is not what you want – you want a life of financial freedom and wealth. So this means that you can't be normal – you are going to have to be unique. I am living an awesome life without debt and there are millions of others who can say the same thing. If you truly want to be wealthy, you must always have more money than you spend. This means not using debt as the answer to a situation that arises. This means waiting until you have cash to pay for an item before you buy it. And this means setting aside money every month (even a small amount in the beginning) and investing it and let it make money for you without you having to do anything but leave it alone. So from this moment on, debt is not an option.

WALKING IN YOUR TRUTH

When I take my car to the mechanic, they can't fix the problem until they know the truth about what is broken. When I go to the doctor, she can't fix my problem until she knows truthfully what it is. If I lie about my symptoms or my situation, she can't help me. The same is true when it comes to your finances and your debt. If you don't know exactly what you owe, you will never be able to set your goals and budget up to eliminate this debt.

The truth will hurt, but it will also set you free. You will never be financially free until you face your debt. And the way to do that is very simple, mechanically speaking. You simply write down each company or person that you owe (you can choose to include your mortgage or not, but you do need to include second mortgages and HELOCS), the amount you pay each month toward that debt and the total balance of each account using a spreadsheet or a legal pad (see the example at the end of this chapter). See how simple that was.

Then comes the hard part – totaling up the account balances and realizing how much of your future is mortgaged because of your debt. But don't be discouraged. What you have just done is a huge step toward wealth – you have acknowledged your reality and now you can fix it. And don't worry if you included everything or not.   In a few weeks, we are going to revisit our debt list and use our credit report to make sure that we have everything written down and accounted for so that we can accurately attack our debt. Also, as you are making your list, you will want to make a separate list for any debts that have gone into collections already. These debts are handled a little bit different when you begin to pay them off.

THE PROCESS

As you begin to set up your budget next week, you will want to make sure that your debt payments are as big as they can be in order to pay off your debt as early as possible. Therefore, I want to take a few minutes and go over the two most used methods for getting out of debt so that you can decide which method will be better for you and set up your game plan accordingly.

Snowball Method – This is the most used and I believe the most effective method and it is the one that I chose to use when I decided to become debt free. The reason that I used it and the reason it is the most popular is because you can get rid of many small debts in a short time frame and therefore, see the progress and stay motivated to carry on and finish your race.

All you do is organize your list of debts from smallest to largest, based on the total balances. Each month you continue to pay the minimum monthly payment on each account in addition to taking any extra money you have and putting it on the smallest account. You do this until that one is paid off. You then take the monthly payment from that account and add it to the extra money each month and put it toward the next account, while still paying the minimum on everything else. Then when that one is paid off, you take the monthly payment from both accounts and repeat the process until everything is paid off. It is called the "snowball method" because each time you pay off a debt, you are adding that money toward the next debt and just like a snowball, with every debt that it paid off, your amount being paid on the debt is bigger and bigger.

This method is designed to keep you motivated. I have many clients using this method who pay off 3 or 4 debts within the first couple of months simply because they begin to budget and focus on getting rid of the debt. Being able to mark off each debt as it gets paid off in a short time will keep you motivated when you hit the larger balances and it takes a little longer. Seeing your progress will carry you through.

Interest Rate Method – Some people attack their debt using the method with the best math. If you choose to use this method, you would arrange your list of debts from the largest interest rate to the smallest interest rate and pay them off in that order. You would still add the paid off debts monthly payment and any extra to the next account just like in the snowball method. However, with this method, you would need to keep yourself motivated and not give up if the debt you are working on is a big debt. For example, if the highest interest rate debt you have is a credit card with a balance of $10,000, it could take you a year to pay that card off. During that year, you will see the balance going down, but that is the only progress you will see and you will need to stay motivated during that time.

Either method brings the same result – you becoming debt free. You need to choose the method that is right for you and your personality. Most people at this point feel beaten up and being able to see the debts disappearing quickly is a great motivator. Just be sure you always keep in mind your main goal – getting rid of your debt and beginning your journey to wealth and financial freedom.

SUMMING UP WEEK 2

This week we identified exactly what debt is and why having debt will not help you to become wealthy or financially free. And since debt is an obstacle in our road to becoming wealthy, we need to stop using it to solve our problems and we also need to get rid of any debt that we may have accumulated in the past.

Therefore, going forward, you are never going to use debt to deal with any circumstances that you may have. I know this can be hard. It may mean that you have to use one car for your family instead of two for a few months. It may mean that you have to use the laundromat for a few months. It may mean that you have to say no to your children when they really want something. But we reap what we sow, and when we sow debt, we are only going to reap payments, never wealth.

You need to sit down and make your list of all of your debts using the example at the end of the chapter. And then you need to decide which method you are going to use to clean up your debts. You need to have all of this information ready for next week as you begin to set up your budget because you will want to squeeze as much as you can out of that budget and put it toward your debt. I know that walking in your truth will be shocking for some, hard and painful, but it will be so worth it. I wish I had a crystal ball and I could show each and every one of you what a life without debt will look like. All I can do is tell you it is worth every bit of blood, sweat and tears that it takes to get there. On to week 3!!

Company Name or Person Owed	Monthly Payment	Balance Owed
Dr. Smith	$ 50.00	$ 3 25.00
Bank of America	$ 25.00	$ 1,428.00
Ford Motor Company	$ 384.00	$ 13,656.28

WEEK 3

SETTING UP A BUDGET AND SPENDING JOURNAL

This is the week that no one wants to do. Many people look at a budget as a prison. But here's the thing – you are going to spend what you spend, but without a budget, you are not going to have any idea what you are spending which is what leads to overspending and debt. If you want to spend $200 on groceries, that's okay as long as you have the money to spend $200 on groceries. And this is what a budget will help you see.

A budget is not a prison – it is a wealth building tool that you need to use to tell your money exactly where you want it to go. Even wealthy people have budgets. If they didn't, they would be broke very quickly. Everyone who is or wants to be wealthy and have money must know and control where their money is going. It is that simple. So, I don't want you to be negative about this week. I want you to look at your budget as the biggest tool you have to become and stay wealthy.

This week, you are going to set up your household budget for next month. There is an example at the end of this chapter as well as a form you can download from our website. You can use whatever format you are comfortable with to set up your budget – it can be our form, your own form or spreadsheet, or a simple legal pad. It doesn't matter how you do it, just that you do it.

✼✼

Many people have no clue exactly what they spend each month in each category. If this is the case for you, you will want to do a spending journal. A spending journal is simply a list of every penny you spend and where you spend it. This will help you to get a realistic picture of your actual spending instead of just guessing at what you spend.

✼✼

One of the hardest parts about doing a budget is getting started. Many people don't know where to start and for the first two or three months, your budget is going to have some mistakes and need a lot of tweaking. The main reason for this is that you probably do not have a realistic view of what you are actually spending per month. This is why for the first couple of months, at least, you will want to keep a spending journal in conjunction with doing a budget. This will help you to get a real look at your actual spending which will help you to budget more accurately as well as help you see where you can cut back in order to get more out of your budget.

THE MECHANICS

Setting up a budget is actually very simple. You write down your income at the top of the page, list your expenses in detailed categories down the page, and subtract the two at the bottom of the page. The goal is to have $0 at the bottom of the page. This is called a "zero dollar budget". The advantage of this budget is that every single dollar gets an assignment and goes where it is told to go. If you have a positive number after subtracting, then you would take that money and assign it to a category – either paying off a debt, savings, or investing (and sometimes a splurge). If you have a negative number after subtracting, then you are either going to have to increase your income or lower your spending in order to get the budget to a $0. If you don't do either one, the only way to make it that month is to use debt and that is no longer an option for you.

This process can take a month or two to iron itself out,

especially if you have been overspending every month. If you need to lower your spending, either to make the bills or simply because you want to put more money toward debt or savings, then you need to analyze each category and see where you can save money. Make sure you shop around in any area that you can (cell phone plans, insurance plans, cable plans, etc.) and that you are getting the best possible price available. You also may have to make the hard decision to give up something for a short while in order to get in a better financial situation. But remember, you are setting yourself up for a better financial situation; therefore, you won't have to stay in this place for long.

The biggest key and the biggest challenge of the budget is being realistic. If you remember, we have used this word in all three weeks so far. And the reason is because until you walk in your truth and face your reality, you will never improve your situation – and this goes for every area of your life, not just money. The good news is that most people within the first few months of doing a budget have actually found extra money. It is amazing how well you can do financially simply by paying attention.

FINAL THOUGHTS ON BUDGETING

- ❖ It is imperative that you do one. You will never have extra money until you control where your money is going. You must be in control of your money and not the other way around.

- ❖ I recommend doing a monthly and a paycheck budget. There is a sample at the end of this chapter of the one that I use that will help you tremendously. You need to lay out your entire month and then distribute your paychecks accordingly.

- ❖ You need to make sure that all of the elements of personal finance are included in your budget - work, spend, save, and give - as well as your financial goals. Most people use the order of spend, save, and then give. Try flipping your order to give, save, and then spend. The formula is the same, but your attitude and thinking will be changed to that of a wealthy person.

- ❖ Make sure you set up a category for miscellaneous or unexpected expenses that might come up. I call this the "G.O.K." (God Only Knows) category on my budget. This category is important because it will keep you from using a credit card or using money from your emergency account for something you overlooked or that came up last minute. You don't need a lot of money in this category – I put about $40 a month in ours – but it can be very helpful when life happens during the month.

- ❖ If you are married, you must do the budget together, even if that means one of you writes it all out and does the math and then shows it to the other. Both of you must have a vote and a voice in where the money goes. And if the budget needs to change during the month, you need to come back together to decide where the changes will be made. Schedule at least one monthly budget meeting during the last week of each month to develop and go over the next month's budget and call mini meetings when "surprises" come up. Use a budget as the marriage saving tool it is known to be.

SUMMING UP WEEK 3

This week is both simple and challenging. From a math perspective, it is simple. But from an emotional perspective, it can be challenging. This week your only goal is to set up next month's budget using whatever form you feel most comfortable with. I realize that this may be the first time some of you have ever even attempted a budget. Do not get discouraged. Simply use the formula – Income – Expenses = $0 – and you are off to a great start. Also, be sure to use a spending journal in conjunction with your budget in order to get a realistic visual of where you spend your money.

For the first several months, especially, your budget will need tweaking many times. And you may even feel like a failure at the end of next month if you didn't stick to your budget or it didn't work out for you. But remember, you are learning something new. Give yourself a break and room for improvement. We will readdress the budget in a few weeks and hopefully by that time you will have a clearer vision of your monthly finances and be able to set up a more accurate budget going forward. On to week 4!

Spending Plan Worksheet

2a. Fixed expenses

Housing
- Rent or Mortgage $ _____
- Insurance/Taxes* $ _____

Utilities
- Telephone $ _____
- Heating $ _____
- Electricity $ _____
- Trash/garbage $ _____
- Water $ _____
- Sewer $ _____
- Cable $ _____
- Other: _____ $ _____

Credit Card Payments
- _____ $ _____
- _____ $ _____
- _____ $ _____

Auto
- Loan payment $ _____
- Insurance* $ _____
- License $ _____

Child Support/Alimony $ _____

Life Insurance* $ _____

Other
- _____ $ _____
- _____ $ _____
- _____ $ _____

Total Monthly Estimated Fixed Expenses $ _____

2b. Controllable expenses

Food
- Groceries $ _____
- Food eaten out $ _____

Household Expenses
- Repairs & supplies $ _____
- Furnishings & appliances $ _____
- Outside upkeep $ _____

Transportation
- Gas and repairs $ _____
- Other transportation $ _____
- _____ $ _____

Personal/Medical Care $ _____

Education/Reading $ _____

Travel & Entertainment $ _____

Child/Elder Care $ _____

Charity/Gifts/Special Expenses $ _____

Clothing $ _____

Savings $ _____

Other $ _____

Total Monthly Estimated Fixed Expenses $ _____

*Monthly portion of premiums if NOT paid by employer OR automatically deducted from your paycheck OR listed with your periodic expenses on page 2.

Reproduced with the permission of Michigan State University Cooperative Extension

WEEK 4

GAINING THE HABITS OF THE WEALTHY

Most wealthy people were not born wealthy. Most of them have gained their wealth through hard work, perseverance, and positive character traits. One of the many positive character traits of a wealthy person is that they have more good habits than bad, especially in the area of money. We all have bad habits, some more than others, but bad habits always get in the way of our success.

This can be especially true in the area of money. If you have lived your life impatiently, then you are going to have the habit of wanting everything right away and not waiting until the right time to purchase it. This habit results in debt and overspending. If you have a negative attitude towards everything and that is your habit, then you will never believe that you can be wealthy; therefore, you won't be. This habit results in staying broke. And there are so many more examples that I could give.

You may be saying "What in the world do my habits, good or bad, have to do with my money?" and my answer is "Everything." Remember, personal finance is 10% math and 90% emotion. The math is easy, but it is the emotions of money that stymie us and keep us from having everything we could have. This book and anything else that I or anyone else ever teaches you will not help you if you don't believe this concept.

So if we understand this, then we realize that a bad habit could be what is in the way of our financial freedom and wealth. I personally had many bad habits in the area of money that I had to overcome and I had to take them on one at a time. I didn't try to eliminate my bad habits – I set out to develop new, good habits to replace the bad ones. Once you begin the process of developing positive habits in the area of money, you will begin to see a positive change in your situation and this will give you the strength and knowledge to change others habits as well.

WHICH ONE?

The first thing you need to do this week is to make a list of your good habits and your bad habits when it comes to money. This includes anything from your attitude to your budget. I want you to list any habit that you can think of, whether good or bad, that affects your finances in any way. This week I want you to focus only on the area of money. You will want to attack other areas later, but right now let's focus on just this one. It may take a few days to get an accurate list so I would say for at least 3 days, this is where your focus should be, just on the list.

After you have made your list, take a long hard look at it and then decide which bad habit you think needs to be replaced first. Which bad habit is preventing you from obtaining your wealth the most? If you have an addiction, overcoming that addiction would probably be the first one you would choose as addictions are not only very harmful to our minds and bodies, but also very costly. The first habit that I chose to change was the habit of eating out all of the time. I had the habit of eating out 3 to 4 times a week which was not only costly to my wallet but also to my waistline. You need to choose the habit that is going to move you forward the most. Changing this first habit is going to be hard and very challenging, but once you see the positive results from making this change, it will give you the encouragement you need to do more. This is one of those times where you just have to do it – no pain, no gain. The end result is always worth it.

Example Costs of Addictions Per Year

- ❖ One cocktail per day with vodka - $ 1300.00
- ❖ One glass of wine per day - $ 1300.00
- ❖ Smoking one pack per day (one person) - $ 1820.00
- ❖ Shopping once a week at mall - $ 10,400.00
- ❖ Marijuana addiction - $ 6200.00
- ❖ 3 sodas per day - $ 1450.00

I'VE PICKED – NOW WHAT?

Studies say that to change a habit takes 21 – 30 days. This timing comes with determination and discipline. Your habit will not go away or be replaced with a new one by magic or simply because you want it to. It is going to take paying attention and great determination to make the change, especially since your old habit will come so easy to you. We tend to always choose the easy way, but this week and over the next several weeks, you are going to have to choose the hard way and not give up.

Remember, you are not trying to remove a bad habit, but rather, you are trying to replace it with a good habit. Every situation is going to be different. You are going to have to make adjustments to accommodate your new habit. And make sure that your adjustments are aggressive enough to guarantee your success in this area.

The habit that I chose to change first was a bad habit that I had of eating out 3 to 4 times a week. First, I had to identify why I did what I did. I ate out mostly for 2 reasons: I didn't like to cook and I really enjoyed the food in restaurants very much. So I had to set up a plan to change this habit as well as a game plan for when the urge came up (and it does a lot, still). First, we lowered our budget for eating out. This meant I didn't have as much money to eat out and I had to live within the reasonable guideline that was set. My new budget only allowed me to eat out 2 times a month which meant I had to eat what I had at home the rest of the time. And when the urge came up to get a pizza or grab Chinese food, I was able to say no because there wasn't any money there for it. Setting up this boundary helped to force me into my new, good habit of only eating out 2 times a month. In the long run, the new, good habit saves me money, allows me to enjoy it more when I do eat out, and helps my waistline.

Just like everything else with personal finance, which habits you change and how you go about changing them is personal. My best advice for you about this week is to be honest about your habits (both good and bad), change them one at a time, and be aggressive with your game plan. And do not take no for an answer – failure is not an option here. You will see a huge, positive change, not only in your finances, but in every area of your life as you begin to transition those bad habits that have held you back to good habits that will move you forward.

SUMMING UP WEEK 4

This week is going to be life changing as you move forward through the process. We don't really realize how our bad habits get in the way of our success. Habits are usually disguised under "that is just the way I am" or "I was born or raised that way". It is extremely freeing to realize that habits can be changed with just a little effort. This gives us motivation to know that we can change our lives and write our story exactly how we want it to look, no matter how we were raised or what we have done in the past.

You need to be honest and realistic this week when you are making your list – with both the good and the bad habits. It is only when we truly see ourselves that we can change and begin to be everything that we want to be. Once you make your lists, be sure to pick the bad habit that is holding you back the most whether it is an addiction, your thinking, your attitude, or something you "inherited" from someone else. And if you are trying to change a habit and you find you cannot do it on your own, there is no shame in seeking help from a professional. You do what you need to do to make the positive changes you need to make in your journey to become wealthy and financially free. On to week 5!

WEEK 5

PREPARING FOR THE EMERGENCIES OF LIFE

My daughter is a Girl Scout and they are always teaching her to be prepared for any situation that may come up. We all need to be like the Girl and Boy Scouts and be sure that we are prepared for any situation that may arise. A large part of being prepared financially is having an emergency fund or an account set up just for such occasions. No matter what your personal situation, there are always going to be things that need to be repaired or replaced or situations, such as a job loss, that you just can't control. But what you can control is how prepared you are for these situations when they occur.

It is not being negative to prepare for emergencies; it is being wise. There are always going to be things that happen in our life that we just can't control, but we can be prepared. Setting up an emergency fund or rainy day fund is the best way to prepare yourself for life when it happens. In the introduction to this book, I talked about how being wealthy means different things to different people. When I set up my emergency fund and had about $2500 in it, I felt the wealthiest that I had ever felt because that was the most money I had ever had at one time and I felt a small sense of financial freedom. I knew that if my car broke down or my washing machine broke, I could get it fixed without much worry. The thing that I realized was that life happens to us whether we are wealthy or whether we are broke. We can't change that, but having money to deal with the problem made that problem a simple inconvenience that I could quickly overcome and forget about instead of a crippling problem that I spent months or years trying to dig out of.

HOW MUCH?

Now that you realize why you need an emergency fund and how having one is a key step to wealth and financial freedom, we need to answer the question "How large of an emergency fund do I need?"

This, just like everything with personal finance, is personal. First of all, there are two types of emergency funds: a starter emergency fund and a 1 year emergency fund. They are both essential to have as soon as you can. What I believe works best is to set up your starter emergency fund as soon as possible and that is what we are going to do this week. Many experts set an amount for this fund at around $1000, but you can make it what makes you feel comfortable. I would make it at least $1000, but you could go as high as $3000. This is what I did because I wanted to be able to cover a car emergency if I needed to. If you are not sure, you could always start at $1000 and raise it at any time if you are still uneasy about the amount.

Your eventual goal is to have a 1 year emergency fund. You can either build this up immediately in continuation to your starter fund or you can build this up after you are out of debt. Again, it is about your budget and your comfort level. You may need to pay off your debt in order to have the money to put in an account or you may be able to adjust your budget or sell something in order to build this up right away. Your end goal on your way to wealth and financial freedom is to be debt free and have an emergency fund of 1 year of expenses set aside. It is only at that point that every dollar you make is yours and you can begin to invest it and let it make money for you. When you reach this point, your money will begin to pay you instead of it being used to pay everyone else.

WHERE DO I PUT IT?

What you are going to do this week is set up a savings account at your bank that is for emergencies only. You need to put as much money in this account as you can in order to get it started. But I want you to start it even if you only have $10. This is just a simple savings account, nothing fancy. The purpose of this account is not to make you money, but to allow you access to it anytime you have a true emergency. I recommend setting it up without any cards attached to it and do not tie it into your checking account. This will remove the temptation to use this account when you are a little short one month. I cannot stress enough – this account is for emergencies only and mishandling your budget is not an emergency, a new pair of shoes is not an emergency, and a new television set is not an emergency. You will be so thankful for this account when your car breaks down or your refrigerator breaks.

When you do have to take money out of this account for a true emergency, you will want to make it a top priority to replace the money as soon as you can. You want to make sure you keep the balance the same as much as possible because sometimes emergencies will come close together.

As I said before, you will want to fill up your emergency fund, whether it is $1000 or $10,000, as quickly as you can. To do this you may have to think outside the box.

There are many ways you can raise the money you need to set up your emergency fund if you don't already have it. Here are just a few examples to get you started:

- *Sell valuable items that you no longer need or want on Ebay and Craigslist.*
- *Clean out every room in your house – make it a family event – and have a yard sale.*
- *Sell a collectible that you have.*
- *Get a part time job*
- *Turn a hobby or craft into a small business*
- *Do odd jobs for the elderly or the wealthy*
- *Clean houses*
- *Walk dogs*
- *Cut grass*
- *Write a book in an area that you are passionate and knowledgeable about.*
- *Teach a class*
- *Tutor*
- *Do mystery shopping*

These are just a few of the hundreds of ideas out there. Be aggressive and make it happen.

You need to keep in mind that what you are doing now is just a season in your life. You won't have to sell everything all the time or you won't have to work two jobs for the rest of your life. You are simply being aggressive and attacking your past in order to have an awesome future. We can do anything for a short while and the end result will be worth it.

SUMMING UP WEEK 5

One thing that I have learned is that life is going to happen to all of us whether we are broke or wealthy. But how we are able to deal with what life dishes out is what makes the difference. "Life is 10% what happens to you and 90% what you do about it." Having an emergency fund is how you deal with the 90% when it comes to money matters. Having money set aside in an emergency fund that you can go to when a situation arises is extremely freeing. It turns a situation into an inconvenience instead of a disaster.

This week you need to set up your emergency fund at your local bank if you don't have a savings account already. You also need to come up with a plan to aggressively add to this account until you have a balance of at least $1000 up to 1 year of expenses.

You are going to be amazed at how wealthy you are going to feel just by having this account set up. On to week 6!

WEEK 6

REVISITING OUR OLD FRIEND – THE BUDGET

It has been three weeks since you set up your budget and your spending journal. At this point, you may have given up or are pulling your hair out, but don't worry. We are going to revisit our old friends and see what we need to do to tweak them and make them work for us. The budget is the biggest wealth building tool we have so it is important to keep using it even when you have a bad month (or two). This is why we are going to spend one more week in this area and hopefully fix any bugs that need to be worked out. This doesn't mean it will be perfect going forward, but hopefully you are building your budget muscle with every month making it easier and easier as you go along.

What I hope you have found out, just by doing a budget for one month is that you may be in better shape than you thought. Many times when people reach out to me, stressed because they can't pay their bills or they are behind several months, all they need is a budget. More times than not, I can set up a budget for them and have them caught up within a month or two and back on track. In addition, many times we find out they actually have money left over every month. I can do this, not because I am a magician or a genius, but simply because I wrote it out and focused on it. Without this great tool and just a little focus, they got behind and overwhelmed. But with it, they found peace and financial freedom and eventually wealth.

YOUR FIRST MONTH

How did your first month go? Whether it went awesome or you struggled, you did it. And that is huge. And problems are going to come, but the good news is they will be less with time. With every month you are going to improve. I hope that you kept a spending journal in conjunction with your budget as we talked about in week 3. This spending journal is going to be key this week in helping you to iron out the wrinkles that are in your budget. If you didn't do a spending journal, no worries; you can do one starting now.

Right now you will want to take time to look back at your spending journal and take every item and put in them in categories such as groceries, eating out, office supplies, medicine, etc. This will give you exactly what you spent last month which will help you decide what amount to put in each category for next month. If you have an item such as stamps or you bought a book, these items would go into the G.O.K. (God Only Knows) category because they are miscellaneous and won't be regular monthly expenses.

LOOKING TO NEXT MONTH

Now it is time to set up your budget for next month. You want to do all of the same things that you did three weeks ago, but with a little more accuracy using your spending journal or your checking account register (if you didn't do a spending journal). This budget should be much closer to your reality than the last one. Make sure you think about your whole month and budget for any special items or one time fees that might be due such as car registration, club dues, magazine renewals, etc.

Make sure that your budget is a zero balance budget just like before. You want this to always be your goal in order for you to know where every dollar is going. The dollars that are unaccounted for are the ones that get away. You can only build wealth if you tell your money where you want it to go. Otherwise, it will choose fun every time. Your budget needs to have a healthy balance between commitments, fun, and wealth building.

And speaking of wealth, now is as good of a time as any to do that tweaking I spoke of earlier. In order to have wealth, you have to have money and especially money that you can invest so that it grows while you live your life. So during this week, I want you to take a long hard look at your budget and be honest about some areas where you might be able to get more money. We will be talking in a few weeks about shopping some of the big items, but this week, let's focus on some small things that can add up at the end of the month.

It is amazing how much you can save based on which grocery store you do your shopping at or just by looking in the sales paper to prepare your menu or by preparing a menu. I still find it so cool when I prepare a menu and make a list for the grocery store, take my little calculator and add everything up and come within 75 cents of my weekly grocery budget. Even now, after 15 years of doing this, I still smile and gloat to my husband. You need to look at saving money as a game instead of a chore. Have fun with it. You don't have to be the coupon queen in order to save money. There are other things just as important that will get you to the same goal. The most important step to saving money is simply paying attention. When we don't pay attention, we just spend money left and right, and at the end of the month look up and ask "where did it go?" When you have a budget, you pay attention and you know where it went.

- Do your grocery shopping at places like Wal-Mart and Aldi or buy store brand wherever you can. They are just as good.
- Go to thrift stores especially on half price day to get great clothes and shoes in new or almost new condition.
- Run your errands while you are on your way to and from work or out for something else.
- Use the energy setting on your appliances
- Wash clothes in cold water
- Unplug electronics when they are not being used including the cords.
- Take your lunch to work
- Rent movies at places like Redbox instead of going to the theatre.
- Make coffee at home instead of buying it at the specialty shops
- Hand wash pots and pans instead of running the dishwasher every night.
- Set your thermostat one degree lower or higher depending on the season.

To take out a family of four to the movies is over $ 65 so you can save $64 just by renting the movies that you want to see. To get coffee 5 days a week is $25 a week so even if you treat yourself once a week, you can save $80 per month. You can save over $50 a month with all of the energy efficient ideas listed above. Are you seeing the point? Paying attention, just a little, can save you a couple of hundred a month.

The biggest struggle people have with budgeting is they see a budget as a piece of paper that keeps telling them what they can't do. But what it really is is a piece of paper that helps you have a balanced life and a life of wealth and financial freedom.

SUMMING UP WEEK 6

This week is all about tweaking and cleaning up your budget and setting up your budget for next month. Next month's budget should include some adjustments that will allow you to either increase your income or decrease your spending so that you have as much money as possible to get out of debt, save for your emergency fund, or begin your wealth building. Remember wealth isn't magic – there isn't a secret formula that only a few have. It is about letting your money make money for you. And in order to do this, you need money to save and invest and the budget is the best place to find what you need. This is the last week that we will be dealing directly with the budget, but you need to make sure that you continue setting up a budget every month before the month starts. And continue to use your spending journal until you have a good grip on your spending and where your money is going. And remember to have a healthy balance in your budget of income, commitments and necessities, fun, and wealth building. It is only with this healthy balance that you will have wealth and financial freedom. On to week 7!

WEEK 7

LEARNING TO USE CASH INSTEAD OF DEBT

As we talked about in week two, wealth has no room for debt. It is impossible to be wealthy as long as you keep paying more for things and keep paying fees for those things. You have obviously chosen a wealthy life instead of a debt filled life if you are reading this chapter. So this week we are going to start our "cash only" life. This means that if you do not have the money for it, you cannot buy it – plain and simple. No matter how much you want it or even need it, no matter what a fantastic bargain it is, you cannot buy anything unless you have the cash to do so. Most of the time, cash is going to be in the form of actual cash or a check. But cash can also refer to debit cards which we will talk about in just a few minutes.

The first thing you need to do this week is take every category in your budget and assign it as either a check or direct bill or a cash envelope item. The only exception might be gasoline because debit can be done directly at the pump. What you will find when doing this is that most of your fixed expenses will be check or direct bill and your controllable expenses will be cash envelopes.

THE ENVELOPE SYSTEM

All of the items that are paid by checks or direct bill are self-explanatory. This just leaves the items that are cash items. With these items, you are going to use a cash envelope system. An envelope system is pretty simple. You just take an envelope – not huge, just big enough to hold cash (the bank envelopes are perfect) – and label it with each of the categories that you assigned to cash a few minutes ago. Then you add up all of the amounts for the cash envelope categories and get that amount out of the bank – either using an ATM card or writing a check – and divide it up among the envelopes. That's it. It really is just that simple.

The cash envelope system may be simple, but it is very effective at keeping you on budget. The main reason is that when the envelope is empty, you are done for the month. You have spent everything that was budgeted for the month in that category. Knowing this causes you to pay attention just a little more. And if you were to have any cash in a category left over at the end of the month, it can either be carried over to the next month or it could be used on a treat. I know wealthy people who still use the cash envelope system long after they become wealthy. The only difference in their envelopes and yours is the amount.

Sample Categories for Cash Envelopes

- ❖ Groceries
- ❖ Eating Out
- ❖ Medicine
- ❖ Entertainment
- ❖ Clothing
- ❖ Gifts
- ❖ Health and Beauty
- ❖ Allowances
- ❖ Zumba (one of mine!)
- ❖ G.O.K. (God Only Knows)
- ❖ Mad Money

DEBIT CARDS

Debit cards are great and should always be used over credit cards. They have the same protection when used as credit and can be used everywhere that a credit card can be used. Sometimes, like for car rentals or hotels, they may hold a little extra – say $100 – but you get it back immediately upon return of the car or settling of your bill.

The danger with using a debit card over cash, however, is overspending. McDonalds did a survey after they added the debit/credit card as a method of payment and found that people spent $2.50 more per transaction. In general, people spend 12-18% more when using debit/credit cards instead of cash. You see, when you pay with cash, you can feel it more than when you just swipe a card. Also, when paying with cash, you have to pay attention to your exact total to make sure you have enough. With a debit card, you just swipe. The best way to stay on budget is to use the cash envelope system with your controllable expenses instead of the debit card, but always use a debit card instead of a credit card.

CASH FILLED LIFE VS. DEBT FILLED LIFE

"Our car broke down this week. I guess we have to go buy a new one now because we can't afford to fix it." This is a statement that I hear a lot. When I am helping people to set up their budget and we get to the auto loan question and they have a payment, 90% of the time it is because they bought a new car when something happened to the old one and they couldn't afford to get it fixed. I am using this as an example to explain the difference in a cash filled life and a debt filled life. When you choose a cash filled life, you begin to become debt free and pile up cash so when something breaks, whether it is your car or your washing machine, you can afford to get it fixed. You only replace something with a new one when it can no longer be fixed and even then you pay with cash and buy only what you can afford.

When you choose a debt filled life, every solution to every problem is debt. When something breaks and you don't have the cash to fix it, you replace it using debt. Then, because of all of the debt you have, when you really do need to replace something because it truly can't be fixed, you still have to use debt. You are a hamster in a wheel.

We have become a replacement society where we used to be a fix it society. When something wasn't working, you called a repairman and they fixed it for you. Nowadays when something breaks, we just throw it out and get a new one. This is true for things, relationships, jobs, and more. But right now, let's focus on things. It is much cheaper to have someone repair your washing machine than it is to replace it. It is much cheaper to have someone repair your car than to replace it.

My van currently has 410,000 miles on it. When it had 340,000 miles on it, the engine went. It cost me $3000 to have it replaced. When this happened, everyone I know asked me what kind of new car I was going to get. They just assumed that because the engine went that that was it. But you see $3,000 is a lot cheaper than $20,000. I didn't need a new car – I just needed a new engine.

I was able to make this choice because I had $3000 in the bank. When you don't have cash in the bank because you have chosen a debt filled life, you do not have the freedom to make the choice I did. If you want to have wealth and financial freedom, you have to start using cash as your only method of payment. Debt is no longer a solution to your problems. And when you make this decision, you will begin to think outside of the box and come up with great solutions for your situations based on the cash you have. There can be no exceptions. It is the only way to reach wealth and financial freedom.

SUMMING UP WEEK 7

This week is all about taking the next step toward a cash only lifestyle and a cash filled life. You have already removed debt as an option early on in week 2. This week has been about taking that one step further and setting up a cash envelope system for your controllable expenses. Using this system instead of your debit card keeps you exactly on budget and keeps you out of debt and on track to wealth. In seven weeks, you have added several important tools to your arsenal to use in your journey to wealth. These tools will help you control your money and know where every dollar is going and will also help you to find extra money to invest in order to become wealthy and financially free. We are one quarter of the way there and I know that you are seeing some very positive changes in your finances already. You have to make sure that you keep doing everything that we talked about as we continue on. You are building a lifestyle much like a snowball. With every week you are gaining more knowledge and more experience and making your life better and better with each passing week. On to week 8!

WEEK 8

PAY ONLY THE TAXES YOU OWE – NO MORE, NO LESS

There are very few things in this world that are a given. Paying taxes is one of them. As a citizen of this great country, you will pay taxes every year so you might as well accept it and stop complaining about it. It doesn't do you any good to get mad at this fact or complain to anyone who will listen – it won't change it. And a negative attitude about anything will stand in the way of your wealth journey; therefore, you will want to keep a positive attitude when it comes to taxes. Knowing what is required of you is the best way to do that. When you know how big the monster is, you can slay it much easier.

So now that you have accepted the fact that you will pay taxes, you want to make sure that you only give the government what you owe them – no more, no less.

WHERE IS MY REFUND?

Billions of dollars are sent out every year by the IRS to individuals in the form of tax refunds. A refund from the IRS is not a gift – it is your money. You will receive a refund from the IRS if you have paid too much money in taxes over the last year, not because the government was being nice and decided to throw a little extra your way. People are always so excited to get their refund every spring, but all they are getting is a check that is paying them back their money at zero percent interest. This is a horrible savings plan.

If you get a refund this year of $3500, this means that you overpaid taxes in the amount of $300 per month. That same $300 per month invested would yield you $4032 in just one year – that is $432 paid to you in interest instead of $0. This is why the IRS savings plan is not the best place to keep your money.

A better plan and what your goal should always be is to break even with the IRS. This is easy to do using a tool that the IRS has available on its website, www.irs.gov. This tool is called a withholding calculator. Here are the steps that you will want to take to see if your withholding status is correct and what it should be in order to break even. You will also use this calculator if you owe money to the IRS every year. Remember, your goal is to break even when it comes to your taxes.

❖ When you go to the withholding calculator on the IRS website, it will ask you multiple questions based on your last pay stub. You can do this process any time during the year to start. Going forward, you will want to do this around the end of January and again in October just to make sure that nothing has changed. This isn't something you do just once and leave it alone. You will want to make this process a step of your yearly financial checkups.

❖ Once you answer all of the questions, the website will give you a tax status for you to give to your employer. This status does not have to match your tax return. For example, if you are married with three kids, your tax return filing status would be married with 5 deductions. But your tax status with your employer may be married with 7 deductions. And that is okay.

❖ You then take the tax status that the calculator gave you and file a new W-4 with your employer. You can either get a form from them or from the IRS website. This will change your federal tax deduction to reflect the correct amount that you owe in taxes. In doing this, you will come within $25 of what you owe as long as you answered everything correctly and nothing changes – like buying a house, having a child, getting married, etc.

Taxes are something that you have to pay, as we said earlier. But you don't want to have the IRS as your banker and you really don't want to owe them anything. By using the withholding calculator, you can either get a raise in your paycheck every pay or you can save thousands of dollars in interest that they will charge when you owe them. Either way, it is more money in your pocket to use toward your wealth building. Remember, it is your money and you want to control it – not the IRS.

✼✼✼

If you are self-employed, the withholding calculator won't work for you. However, you can get just as close and avoid the same issues as everyone else. For every dollar you make, make sure you keep out a percentage for taxes. For an average person, this would be about 25% - it should equal your tax rate. This tax money should be kept in a separate account just for taxes so that you have it when the time comes. The IRS wants self-employed people to file estimated tax forms each quarter. This is a great way for you to keep your taxes in line and to avoid the penalties for owing too much at the end of the year. Just like an employee would do, you need to use the tools provided by the IRS to get as close as you can to the exact amount you owe. And doing an estimated tax form and payment quarterly will help you do this.

✼✼✼

This week, your only focus is to get your filing status correct and set yourself up to break even with the IRS. We all know that the government is not known for handling money very well so we want to make sure that we give them only what we are required to give them – no more, no less.

I OWE THE IRS – NOW WHAT?

Just like there are billions of dollars in refunds sent out each year, there are also billions of dollars owed in taxes every year. This is a position that you do not want to find yourself in. The IRS has the power to garnish wages and levy accounts without due process unlike corporations who have to get a judgment first. Basically, the government has the power to take what is owed to them and they will get it one way or the other. This is why it is extremely critical that you use the withholding calculator or estimated taxes process to know what you are going to owe and make sure that you pay it.

A huge mistake that I made and that many people make is that they do not even file their tax returns because they think they are going to owe money. This only makes matters worse. First of all, it is illegal to not file a tax return and not filing can come with a jail sentence if not dealt with. Secondly, as I said before, you won't know how big the monster is until you file. You cannot avoid paying your taxes, no matter how hard you try and trying to do so will cause you nothing but a life of stress and pain. Therefore, the best thing you can do for yourself and your finances is to make sure you are always up-to-date with the IRS.

However, if you find yourself in this position, you will want to file any tax returns that have not been filed immediately. This is your first step and your only priority. If after doing so, you find that you do owe money and you cannot pay, then you will want to set up an installment agreement with the IRS and make payments until you pay what you owe. The payments you will make not only include what you owe, but interest and penalties as well. You will want to make paying this money back a top priority above all other debts you may have and make sure you never owe them again. Do not choose to avoid the issue. I will say it one more time – just in case you don't believe me. The IRS will get the money you owe them, every penny, no matter what. You cannot negotiate with them or make a deal. The only thing you can do is pay it off as quickly as possible and never owe them again.

SUMMING UP WEEK 8

The most important thing you need to take away from this week is that you will pay taxes and you can do this either the easy way or the hard way. Part of being a wealthy person is making sure that you always take care of business and filing and paying your taxes is the most important business of all. This week you have two things to do: make sure that all of your tax returns are filed and current and to use the withholding calculator to determine your correct tax status with your employer. You will always have to pay taxes whether you are broke or wealthy, but you only want to give them what you owe – no more, no less. This allows you to keep everything else and use it to live and to invest for your future which will lead you to wealth and financial freedom. On to week 9!

WEEK 9

OBTAINING AND UNDERSTANDING YOUR CREDIT REPORT

Wealthy people always know everything about their money and their finances. This includes knowing what is on their credit report. Whether you have a zero credit score, a high credit score, or you are somewhere in between, you need to know what is on your credit report even though you aren't using credit anymore and you are getting out of debt. People always tend to think of their credit score simply in terms of whether they can borrow money or not, but there is more to it than that. Your credit report is also a visual aid of your finances – whether you are true to your word and how you treat your money. It is your financial reputation so to speak. Therefore, you want to make sure that your reputation is being represented accurately and in the best light possible.

THE CREDIT REPORT

There are three main credit reporting agencies that companies use – Experian, TransUnion, and Equifax.

Companies who use these reporting services report both the good and the bad about your relationship with them. Most of the time the information that they report is accurate, but sometimes it is not. This is the reason you will want to obtain your free credit report from each agency each year.

You are allowed one free credit report from each of the three companies once a year. You can get a credit report anytime – you will just have to pay if you get more than one per agency per year. You should get one from each of the three companies every 4 months. For example, you could get one from Experian in April, one from Equifax in August, and one from TransUnion in December. This way you spread them out and you cover each company once a year because sometimes something may be on one and not on the others.

You want to make sure that you get your report from a free source such as www.annualcreditreport.com or directly from the reporting agency. You never need to pay a monthly fee for a report or to have someone monitor your account for you. Monitoring is easy and free and something you can do yourself.

Whenever you receive your report, you will want to look it over carefully and make sure that everything on it is accurate. If an item is not accurately reported, you can dispute it and have it removed. But you can only do this if a company is not reporting the truth. If you are behind in payments or you went into collections on an account, you cannot dispute this just because you don't want it reported. You can only dispute true inaccuracies. Each of the three companies has a different process for disputes so you will want to check with them on what exactly you need to do if you find an inaccuracy.

This week you will want to obtain a credit report from one of the three agencies so that you can get an exact picture of where you are financially and to make sure that everything has been reported accurately. Also, next week, we will be using this report to update your debts to exactly what you owe and divide them into two categories: current and collections. You never want to obsess over your credit report or your credit score, but you do want to be diligent and make sure that your report is accurate and a realistic visual of your financial situation.

THE CREDIT SCORE

It seems like every time we talk about money, we end up talking about our credit score. Is your credit score as important as everyone makes it out to be? Credit scores are used for many different things – the main one being for credit/debt. And since we are not using debt anymore, it would seem logical that our score doesn't matter. And in truth it doesn't. But remember, your credit report including your score is a representation of your financial situation; therefore, you want to have a good report. A good credit score is either a score above 700 (this may vary with each lender) or a zero credit score. Yes, I said a zero credit score. This is what your score will be if you get out of debt and never go into debt again and it can be just as powerful as a high credit score.

Your credit score is figured out as follows:

- ❖ 35% payment history
- ❖ 30% amounts owed
- ❖ 15% length of credit history
- ❖ 10% new credit
- ❖ 10% types of credit used

Do you notice the common theme throughout this formula? It is credit/debt. You must use credit/debt in order to have a credit score, but you do not need to be in debt to have a credit score. As we talked about in week 2, there are some wealthy people who use credit/debt (the bank's money) instead of their own money to buy larger items or they use a credit card for purchases and pay it off every month. This technically isn't debt because they have the money to back it up. But you cannot be in debt and be wealthy. I always recommend aiming for the zero credit score, but if you choose to keep a credit score, aim high by getting out of debt and paying off in full monthly any credit cards you may use.

A Zero Credit Score Life

A zero credit score is just as powerful as a high credit score. When someone sees that you have a zero score, they know that you must have money because you do not have debt. And as hard as it may be to believe, you can even buy a house with a zero credit score. It is a little harder and takes a little bit longer to get approved because you have to get manual approval (the way it was done many years ago), but you will probably have more success and end up with a lower rate especially if you have a great job history and rental history. There are only a few companies who do manual mortgage underwriting, but it is possible. If you have a lower credit score, it will take a few years to get to a zero credit score because you will have to pay everything off first and it may take time for everything to clear off completely. But for me, it is the way to go.

The main thing I want to say about credit scores is this: Don't put all of your focus on them and your energy worrying about what your score is. The change in this country's personal debt problem coincided with the establishment of the FICO scoring system. Even though FICO has been around since the 1950's, it wasn't used as the primary credit decision maker until much later. And now, every bit of debt you have is solely based on your FICO score. And because of this, people live by their scores. We are even teaching our kids today that you have to have a credit score, but we don't teach them what this means. Remember, to have a credit score, you must have credit/debt. Know what that looks like and know what that means, and then make your decision. Is it worth your wealth to have a great credit score?

HOW TO HAVE YOUR CAKE AND EAT IT TOO

Have you ever noticed how older generations have more money and younger generations have more stuff? This is because the older generations grew up in a time where they learned to use a credit card without using debt or they learned to buy a house and pay it off in ten years instead of thirty. Younger generations learn to use credit cards and debt to get what they want now whether they have the money or not and then find themselves not being able to pay it back. A great example of this is the student loan debt in this country and how many young people struggle for 10-20 years after they graduate trying to pay the loans back.

In order to be wealthy, we need to learn from and emulate wealthy people. Wealthy people have high credit scores and no debt – they have their cake and eat it too. This is the goal that we all need to have. They are able to accomplish this because they have the discipline and the habit of paying off a credit card every month if they use it. They have the discipline and the habit of never borrowing money that they do not have. They only borrow when it is financially sound. For example, they may borrow to buy a house even though they have the cash to pay for it. They can borrow the money at 3.5% instead of using their money and losing 10%. In addition, they put down a large down payment and pay it off as quickly as possible saving them even more money. Doing this gives them a great credit score and wealth at the same time.

All of us want to be able to have our cake and eat it too, just like wealthy people. But you also want to be realistic about your situation. I was one of the younger generations who used a credit card with every intention of paying it off every month, but something always came up. I wasn't able to follow through with my intentions because I didn't have the cash to pay for it; therefore, I should have never bought it in the first place. I had to be realistic about myself and realize that the best thing for me was to not have any credit cards and just use cash or my debit card for everything I bought because it had the same coverage and benefits of a credit card without the debt. This decision is what brought me to a zero credit score instead of trying to maintain a high credit score and tempting myself. This was a habit that I developed and even though now I could handle a credit card, I don't need one and I live a great life without one.

This is a decision that you will have to make based on your personality and your discipline level. Just be honest and make the choice that is best for you – no credit and a zero credit score or credit that is paid off monthly or early and a high credit score. Just remember your goal – to be wealthy and financially free. You may have to take a different path than other wealthy people, but as long as you get there, that is all that matters. Just be honest about the habits you have formed and either work with them or defeat them all the while keeping your eye on the main goal.

SUMMING UP WEEK 9

Everyone is always talking about credit scores and how everybody needs one. But as I have tried to show this week, it is not necessary to have one in order to function in this world. However, your credit score along with your credit report is a representation of your financial reputation and that is something that you always want to keep on the positive side. Your only task this week is to obtain your free credit report from the website mentioned before or directly from the reporting agencies. At this time, you only need to get one and I would start with Equifax as it is the most used. You can obtain the other ones every few months the way we talked about or you can get them all at once if you wish. Once you receive your report, you will need to go over it with a fine toothed comb and make sure there are no errors that need to be disputed. If there are, you will need to do this immediately, directly with the reporting agency (i.e.

Equifax), not with the lender or collection agency. Having this credit report will give you an honest look at your financial situation and help you know exactly what you need to take care of in order to clean up the past. Cleaning up the past and moving on to bigger and better things is a huge step in becoming wealthy and financially free. On to week 10!

WEEK 10

REVISITING YOUR DEBT

I hope at this point, 2 ½ months into your wealth journey, you have learned a lot and are seeing progress – not only in your thinking, but in your finances as well. Remember that the goal you are aiming for is to set yourself up in the next 16 weeks to be able to act and think like a wealthy person which will eventually result in wealth and financial freedom for you. At this point, you may be wishing for that magic pill that makes you wealthy instantly, but there is no such thing. You may have gotten a late or slow start, but you are going to have a great finish. But you have to hang in until the end – and beyond.

One of the biggest obstacles standing in your way of being wealthy is your debt – there is no way that you can keep your debt and become a wealthy person. As long as you are spending more than you make and giving your money away to banks and corporations, there will be nothing left over for you to save and invest and build wealth. This is not just an opinion – it is a mathematical fact. As I am writing this, the government is in day one of a government shutdown and one of the reasons for this shutdown is that they have spent more than they have made which causes them to have to keep borrowing and keep raising the debt ceiling. They have the same problem that many people do – they simply spend more than they make and this will make you broke every single time.

But you want to be wealthy and financially free or you wouldn't be reading this book. This means that you don't want to be broke anymore and live like a broke person which means getting rid of your debt and never going into debt again. In week two, we talked about what debt is and how stopping all debt is a must. During the last eight weeks, I hope you have resisted the temptation to use that credit card or overdraft protection or any other form of debt as a solution for payment. We also talked a little about how to get out of debt and I showed you two different methods that are used when deciding which debt to tackle first. Getting out of debt is going to be a process – it will not happen overnight. But you have to keep going. If you keep going and do not go any further into debt, you will be out of debt eventually, even if you only make minimum payments, but of course, you want to do more than that to speed up the process.

PRAISING YOUR PROGRESS

Have you made any progress in the last eight weeks? If you have small debts, you probably did and if your debts are larger, you may not have. You want to make sure that you always praise your progress even if it is just a few dollars. Any progress is still progress and since you are not going further into debt, it means that you are better off today than you were yesterday. I recommend, when we are done with this week, that you take your debt list, as scary as it may be, and post it somewhere where you and your spouse can see it. Then as you pay each debt off, take a big fat magic marker and mark it off. If for any reason you only have large account balances left, then take a marker and change the balance once a month so you can see your progress. Sometimes, when all you see are bills coming in, it is hard to see any success and you will tend to lose motivation. You must stay motivated during this process and one thing you will find as you go along is that the more success you see, the more you will do. If you were on a diet and never lost any weight, you would stop dieting. It is the same with getting out of debt. If you can't visually see progress, you will give up and never reach your goal of wealth and financial freedom.

What Success Really Means

Success isn't just reaching your goal. It is also what you do along the way. Zig Ziglar said it best - "Success is the doing, not the getting; in the trying, not the triumph. Success is a personal standard, reaching for the highest that is in us, becoming all that we can be. If we do our best, we are a success." You are a success already by just what you have done in the last ten weeks. It means that you are brave enough to take the steps necessary to fix your past financial mistakes, learn from them, and be all that you were born to be. You are a success!

ATTACKING THE DEBT

Now that you have a copy of your current credit report, you are going to be able to make an accurate and realistic list of all of your debts. Using your debt list from week two and your credit report, you need to make a new debt list that will include every single thing you owe. If you have current debts and debts in collections, you will want to make two lists and separate them out. You always want to work on the current debts first and let sleeping bears sleep as long as you can. Once you pay everything off that is current, then you can attack the old debts that are in collections and settle with them, which we will talk about in detail in a moment.

If at any point while you are paying off your current debts a sleeping bear wakes up, you will just need to deal with it the way you will learn in a moment and go back to the current debts. Focus is very important always; therefore, you don't want to be distracted by too many things while you are attacking your debt. If something from the past comes up, deal with it and get back on track as soon as possible.

This week so far you have updated your debt list to reflect items that have been paid off and items that were on your credit report that you may have forgotten about. Just a reminder from week 2, you do not include your mortgage on this list of debts. HELOCs and second mortgages, however, should be included. You have also praised your progress and learned how to stay motivated during this process. That is really what this week is all about and I would recommend you do this every few months or so in order to get an accurate picture of where you are.

I do want to cover one more thing this week and that is how to settle your old debts. At any time during this 26 weeks and beyond, you may be faced with a collection situation that needs to be handled and I want to make sure you have the knowledge you need to handle it. The settlement process, if not needed before then, will be needed once you get everything on your current list paid off.

SETTLING OLD DEBTS

You want to make sure that you settle every debt that you have either by paying it off in full or making a deal with the collector. You cannot make a deal on current debts – only debts that are in collections. This doesn't mean that you put your debts in collections on purpose just so you can settle them for less. But the reality is that sometimes life happens or we make wrong decisions and we find ourselves in a pickle. You want to make sure if you find yourself in this position that you handle it properly so that it doesn't come back to haunt you at the most inopportune time.

The first thing you need to know about settling old debts is your rights as a consumer. Yes, you owe the money, but this doesn't give anybody the right to mistreat, verbally abuse or threaten you. I recommend that you read over the Fair Debt Collection Practices Act and familiarize yourself with all of your rights. This will detail when people can call you and how many times a day – things like that. Also, you do not have to answer the phone when they call. Yes, it is annoying as all get out when they call once or twice a day, but it is easy to let them leave a message, listen to it and erase it. You shouldn't avoid the problem, but you shouldn't allow them to mistreat you either. If they are calling you at work, you have the right to tell them not to bother you at work and if they continue, you can report them to the Federal Trade Commission. The best thing for you is to know your rights (i.e. they can't send you to jail), tolerate them as long as they are just doing their job, and report them if they become harassing or abusing. Again, you do owe the money and you haven't paid. Their job is to collect it from you. They are just doing their job, but if it gets out of hand, you have someone to go to to report them.

When you have a debt go into collections, how persistent the collector is is usually based on the amount owed. If you only owe a few hundred dollars, they probably won't be very pushy. However, if you owe thousands or tens of thousands, they will probably make your life a living mess. It will start with phone calls and letters, hopefully offering you options for settling with them. But if you continue to not pay them, they will, more than likely, eventually sue you. Now, this isn't as bad as it sounds. Basically, they do this because they haven't gotten anywhere with the calls and letters so they will ask a judge to step in and order a judgment in order to make you pay. If you haven't taken it seriously up to this point, you will definitely want to take it seriously now because with a judgment they can garnish your wages and use other legal means to get their money.

If you have a debt that goes this far, you will want to stop paying extra on anything else and deal with it as soon as you can. The bad news is they sued you – the good news is that now there will be a lawyer to contact to work something out instead of a collector. You will want to work some sort of reasonable settlement out with them in order to put this behind you. You do not need a lawyer yourself as it is a pretty cut and dry process; just work with the lawyer assigned from the collector and try to make some sort of deal. Never promise money you don't have, but be aggressive in your thinking and work extra or sell something to make the deal happen.

Many debts will not get to this point. Most of your collections debts can be settled directly with the collector before they get this far, as long as you don't avoid them forever. Listed below are the steps in settling a debt with a collector. This is something you can do yourself – you do not need to hire a company or debt consolidation firm to help you. It is a simple process that you can do and save a lot of money. You want to make sure that you maintain control of your financial situation. Here's all you do:

1. List your collections debts in order from smallest to largest. You will want to get the little ones out of the way as soon as possible so you can attack the big ones as soon as you can.
2. Between what you owe and the amount of money you have, decide on a reasonable offer to make the company to settle the debt. These collectors are usually buying these debts for seven to ten cents on the dollar so I would say around 25 cents on the dollar is a good starting point.
3. Contact the current holder (collector) of the debt. You can find this out from your credit report or from any recent correspondence you may have received regarding the debt. Make absolutely

sure you are dealing with the current holder because if it is an older debt, it may have had several collectors over the years. You can either make your offer in writing or over the phone, but you must receive the collector's confirmation of the agreement in writing – this is a must. Never send money to anyone you are settling a debt with without a letter of agreement from them in writing.

4. The process of coming to an agreeable amount may take a few tries. At the end of this chapter is a sample of a debt settlement letter that you can use. Basically, you give them your situation, let them know that you only have so much money to settle with and you will be doing so in the order in which companies reply. If they drag their feet or get uncooperative with you, then move on to the next one and come back to them. You should be reasonable since, as we said before, you do owe the money, but there is no reason to become a slave to their dragging their feet.

5. Once you receive the confirmation of the deal in writing from the company, you then send them a money order or cashier's check for the agreed upon amount. **Never** give them access to your

banking information or set up payment plans of automatic withdrawals. If you do this, they will clean out your account and you won't be able to get your money back because you owe them the money. There is something very important to remember in this process. You are asking them to do you a favor and accept less than you owe because you were unable to pay the full amount. This is not something that they have to do, but most are willing to do it just so they can get some of their money back. You made a commitment to pay them what you borrowed and you weren't able to fulfill that commitment. Be humble and work with them as much as they will allow you to, but never accept disrespect, threats or verbal abuse.

6. Once you have done everything above and the deal is done, you need to staple a copy of the money order or check to the letter and keep it in a file forever. Yes, I said forever. There are collection companies out there who buy debt that has already been settled and try to collect again and sometimes there are bookkeeping errors. You are dealing with humans and humans make mistakes. This is one area where you don't want any misunderstanding. By

keeping this information, if you are ever contacted again about this debt, you will have proof of payment and evidence to use in asking that it be removed from your credit report immediately. Without this information, you cannot report any misunderstandings or problems because you will not have proof that you took care of it.

Settling your debts is a part of your financial reputation. In doing so, you are showing that, even though you made some mistakes and went through some hard times, you persevered and made it through. It is a sign of great integrity to pay everyone what you owe them and it shows that you follow through on your commitments, no matter how long it takes.

SUMMING UP WEEK 10

This week is all about setting yourself up to get completely out of debt. Debt will never bring you wealth; therefore, getting out of debt is a major key to wealth. One of the common characteristics of millionaires is integrity. Paying off and settling your debts put you in that category. You are following through with your commitments, even if it is years later, and you are making it right. True integrity leads to wealth and financial freedom. And don't forget to celebrate and embrace your success and progress. Anything you are doing that is making a positive difference in your financial life is success and needs to be celebrated. Persevere and you will reach your ultimate goal of wealth and financial freedom.

September 18, 2013

Bank of America

Collections Department

P.O. Box 1234567890

Anywhere, USA 12345

Dear Sir or Madam,

I am contacting you regarding account number _____. After some financial hardship, I am now in a position to satisfy the debt on the above account number. I would like to ask for your cooperation in helping to resolve this debt. I am putting forth a sincere effort to settle my debts and pay them off.

I would like to propose a full payment toward this debt in the amount of $ _____. I propose that this amount be accepted as payment in full without recourse for this debt. In addition, I would like to request that all late payment remarks or charge-offs be removed from my credit bureau reports.

I am currently working cooperatively with several additional creditors for debt settlement purposes, and therefore, my funds are limited. For this reason, I am settling those debts which can be satisfied through written settlement proposals, such as I am proposing to you today, in the order that I receive them until my funds are depleted.

A couple of my creditors have already made acceptable settlements with me. I would like to include this debt among them. If the above proposal is acceptable, I will pay the agreed upon balance in full using a money order or cashier's check as soon as I receive a copy of this agreement in writing from you. I will not send any money until I receive this document. Upon receipt of the signed agreement, I will send you the agreed upon funds immediately and will consider this account as paid in full. Thank you for your time and swift response to this issue. Have a blessed day!

Sincerely,

Debbi King

P.O. Box 1234567890

Anywhere, USA 12345

215-555-5555

CHECK IN TIME

Well, here we are at the end of 10 weeks. I know you are noticing a difference in your finances already and I just wanted to take a minute to recap everything we have talked about so far and make sure we are at the same place in your wealth journey.

- ❖ You should have written down your 3 year goals in 7 different areas of your life: career, family & friends, marriage & relationships, personal growth, spiritual, physical health, and financial. This will help you know what you are looking to accomplish and improve over the next 3 years and help you take the necessary steps today to get there.

- ❖ When it comes to the area of debt, we know that debt will never bring you wealth. Therefore, you should have stopped using debt of any kind and developed an envelope system and a cash only system for your finances. At this point you also should have also gotten a free copy of your credit report and used it to make a list of your current and your collections debts. You will have noticed some progress and lowering of your balances over the last ten weeks as you are not adding to the balances and hopefully you have come up with a little extra each month to attack the debt list.

- ❖ You also should have set up a monthly budget and spending journal. You have had 2 months of budgeting and you are getting ready to do a third. Between your old budgets and your spending journal, you should be getting to the point where your budgets are accurate and realistic. Writing everything down and getting a snapshot of your finances for each month will definitely help you to not overspend and continue to need debt to make it.

- ❖ You have already replaced one bad money habit that was bringing you down with a new good money habit. It has been six weeks of working on the new habit so you are probably in a place where you can begin replacing another bad money habit with a new good one while you are still getting stronger with the first one.

- ❖ You should have an emergency fund set up and hopefully you have been able to put at least

$1000 into it at this point. If not, that's okay. Just continue to save and sell and build that account up as quickly as you can.

❖ One way that you could have found some extra money for your budget, your debt, and your savings account is when you checked your withholding status with the IRS. At this point, you should have your withholding status with your employer at exactly what it should be by using the withholding calculator on the IRS's website. Remember, in doing this, you should come within $25 or so of exactly what you owe.

The first ten weeks have probably been a little crazy and somewhat overwhelming. You are doing things that possibly you have never done or even knew how to do. But everything that you have done to date is something that wealthy people do each and every day. What you were doing before wasn't working or you wouldn't need this book. Albert Einstein defines insanity as doing the same thing over and over and expecting different results. You have stopped the insanity by trying something new and something that is not only going to work today, but forever. You are building wealth and financial freedom every day, even when you can't see it. On to week 11!

WEEK 11

GETTING RID OF THE CRUTCHES

About a year ago, my daughter hurt her knee and had to use crutches for about 3 weeks. When she went for one of her checkups, the doctor told her to keep the brace on, but to stop using the crutches. This didn't make her happy at first because she didn't have anything to lean on when her knee began to bother her and become uncomfortable. But after a few days, she began to be more comfortable and her knee became stronger and stronger because she wasn't using her crutches – she was relying on her own strength.

What are you leaning on? What are your crutches when it comes to your finances? This week we are not only going to identify them, but we are going to remove them. I know that you are just as apprehensive as my daughter was, but just like her, you will never build your wealth muscles as long as you are relying on your crutches to hold you up.

CREDIT CARDS

Credit cards are the ultimate crutch if you are not able to pay off your balance at the end of every month. As we have discussed before, wealthy people have credit cards that they use for convenience and pay off at the end of every month. Therefore, credit cards themselves are not the issue. However, when you are using them to buy something before you have the money or you are using them to get through month to month, then they are crutches and are definitely going to hinder your progress.

There is nothing wrong with cutting up a credit card and this is exactly what we are going to do this week. As a matter of fact, you are going to cut up all of your credit cards this week. You may be thinking that your credit cards are not a crutch for you, but if you carry a balance and have debt on them, they are. The best thing for your wealth building is going to be to cut them up and get rid of them. And there is no need to have a credit card because you are now using your debit card or cash for every purchase you make.

Debit cards can be used everywhere that a credit card can be used and carries with it the same coverage as a credit card if there is a fraudulent charge against it. Many debit cards even have reward programs attached to them. So if you are carrying around that credit card just to rack up the miles, let it go. You should never hold on to a credit card and carry a balance just for a few points that you may never use.

The first step and most important step is to cut up all of your credit cards. But you will also want to close all of these accounts as well. Yes, I said close the accounts. The reason is that if they stay open, they are still a crutch to you because when you are in a bind, you will be tempted to call them and get another card issued. If the account is closed, it removes the crutch completely which is the goal. You cannot do things halfway and expect full results. If you want to experience wealth and financial freedom, you must go all the way. And this really shouldn't be a problem if you are fully committed to being wealthy because you will not need debt anymore.

One concern many people have is how closing all of your accounts will affect your credit score. Closing your accounts will have a small effect on your credit score, but as long as you keep making the payments on time, it will have very little effect. And once you pay the credit cards off, they will disappear completely from your credit report anyway. People who are too dependent on their crutches tend to come up with many excuses to keep them, even if these crutches are preventing them from getting what they really want. An excuse is just a reason to keep doing what you are doing. You either really want to be wealthy or you don't. Credit cards and carrying a balance will never get you there. Therefore, it is very simple – if you want to be wealthy, you will cut up your credit cards and close the accounts and use debit cards and cash going forward – period.

OVERDRAFT PROTECTION

Overdraft protection is another major crutch that people have and one that you must get rid of if you have it. Overdraft protection on a banking account, such as a checking account, is not free money nor is it a cushion that the bank gives you "just in case". Overdraft protection is a crutch and a very expensive one at that. It used to be that you could only get overdraft protection on your account if you had good credit – it was basically a credit line that the bank approved you for in case of an overdraft. However, then and now, this protection came at a very high price. Several years ago the banking policies changed and banks started giving everyone overdraft protection unless you opted out of it – the complete opposite of the old way. The reason that they changed their tune was they saw just how much money they could make on this "service".

Overdraft protection is there to cover every transaction that you do not have the cash for – for the price of around $35 a pop. You could realistically end up paying $80 for $10 worth of stuff. I've seen it happen. You need to remove this crutch completely. All you have to do is call your bank or visit your local branch and tell them that you want to opt out of the overdraft protection on every account of yours that they have it on. They will try to persuade you to keep it by letting you know that any transaction that you try will be declined if you don't have the money. Well, duh. If you don't have the money, then the transaction should be declined. If you keep track and balance your checkbook, this should never be a problem. And this way, if you are declined, you know there is a problem and you can look into it right away.

Remember one thing – one of the three ways that banks make money is on fees. Therefore, they are going to want as many fees as they can to make the most money that they can. This means that you need to protect yourself from having to pay unnecessary fees and one way to do this is by removing this crutch from your accounts. This means checks and debit card transactions – all transactions. Just like credit cards, there is no middle ground here. The banks are salespeople – they will say everything they can to get you to keep this "service" because without you, they can't make any money. Just politely ask them to remove this protection from everything you have and know that you have done the best thing for your wealth and financial freedom.

Crutches are simply symbols of anything that you rely on and lean on too much – so much so that they become harmful instead of helpful. The two crutches above are just two examples that most people have. However, crutches can also be bad habits, addictions, people, stagnant jobs, etc. Therefore this week we are going to do two very important things: remove both of the crutches listed above, if you have them, and list anything else that is a crutch for you and remove it. Some crutches take time to remove and that is okay.

Identifying them and being realistic about them is a huge step in removing them so that nothing stands in your way to wealth and financial freedom.

SUMMING UP WEEK 11

Just like my daughter had to stop using her crutches in order to become stronger, you have to stop using any crutches that you have been using when it comes to your finances in order to become stronger financially. The purpose of a crutch is to hold you up for a short time until you can get stronger and healed from your injury. No one ever keeps crutches for the rest of their life after an injury. You have been using credit cards and overdraft protection, as well as other things, to hold you up because you weren't strong enough or knowledgeable enough to do it on your own. But now you are – you know what you need to do and you are strong enough to do it.

You must cut up all of your credit cards, close the accounts and remove your overdraft protection from your banking. You need to do this this week. Stop making up excuses and telling yourself all of the reasons why you shouldn't do it. Yes, it will be scary at first because you have relied on these crutches to hold you up for far too long. So just like my daughter, you are not going to want to stop using them or remove them. But you must. Look at me as your financial doctor. I know what you are going through, but I also know where you want to be and what you need to do to get there. Trust me, as someone who has been exactly where you are and who has walked in your shoes. Instead of helping you, your crutches are preventing you from having the wealth and financial freedom that you desire. Remove the crutches and be wealthy. On to week 12!

WEEK 12

SHOPPING AROUND FOR THE BEST

"15 minutes can save you 15% on car insurance." This is so true. And not only can you save on car insurance, but you can save in other areas of your finances as well with just a few minutes of your time. As common sense will tell you, the less money you spend, the more money you will have. This doesn't mean you have to go without. You can accomplish this goal by shopping around and getting the most for your money in all areas of your financial life.

This week we are going to talk about the areas of your budget that can be shopped and how you can get the most out of every dollar in every area. This week isn't about saving a few dollars at the grocery store or saving money by taking your lunch to work – those are also important. But this week is about bigger savings in the areas that we take for granted. You don't have to stay with the same company and pay whatever they charge you when it comes to things like auto insurance and cell phones. Every time your contract or policy is up, shop around and find the best deal going. Just a little bit of time and a few phone calls can save you hundreds of dollars a month. Let's look at some of these areas and go over exactly what you can do and changes you can make to get those savings that you need.

AUTO (AND ALL) INSURANCE

You need to shop all of your insurances – auto, health, life, etc. – to make sure that you are getting the most coverage for the lowest dollar. However, this is an area where you need to make sure that you don't have more coverage than you need. Also, make sure that you don't have any "gimmick" insurance policies such as cancer insurance or pet insurance. These policies are considered gimmick because they are not necessary and odds of you needing them are very slim. For example, what cancer insurance covers is what health insurance and long term disability insurance cover. Health and long term disability insurance are necessary, cancer insurance is not. Remember insurance companies have to make money in order to pay out claims; therefore, you will probably pay in more than you will take out. So instead of buying pet insurance and never using it, just put a little extra away every month into your emergency fund and then you will have what you need, if and when something happens to your pet.

The best way to do insurance shopping is through an independent insurance agent. They do all of the work for you and find you the best deal from all of the companies out there – companies you may not even know exist. For example, my current auto insurance company is a company that I had never heard of before, but is one of the highest ranking insurance companies out there. They get all of their business from independent guys and not directly with the consumer. This saves them advertising dollars and much more so that they can pass the savings on to you. But when you need them, they are there for you just like a "well known" company would be. You don't want to pay for a name, you want to pay for service and your local independent insurance agent can help you with this.

Also, make sure that you are getting the best coverage for you and your money. For example, you would want to choose term life insurance instead of whole life, in most cases. Term will give you the best coverage for the lowest price. An example of a good money decision when it comes to your auto insurance is if you don't have enough money in your emergency fund to cover the cost of a nice used car should something happened to yours and it was your fault, you would want to add

Whole vs. Term Life Insurance

I just wanted to take a minute and describe both types of life insurance so that you can see why, in most cases, term is better than whole.

Whole life insurance works like this. You buy a policy for, let's say, $250,000. You will pay, on average, around $250 per month for this coverage. This policy pays the same upon death as a term life policy does. The only difference is that most whole life policies have a cash value which is like a savings account you can borrow against. However, when you die, your beneficiaries do not receive the extra cash value of the plan. They would simply get $250,000. And, if you have borrowed against the policy, and die before it is paid back, the amount you owe would be deducted from the $250,000.

Term life insurance, however, would be about $20 per month for $500,000 up to $1,000,000 in coverage, based on your age and your health. So for around 90% less per month in premium, you would receive, at least, double the amount of coverage. Now, if you wanted, you could invest the $230 difference in premiums per month into a good growth stock mutual fund and when you die, you would have around $300,000 extra that your beneficiary would inherit because it is your money.

As you can see, from a cost benefit point of view, term life insurance is always going to be better. However, if for any reason you cannot get term life insurance, but you can get whole life insurance, whole life is better than no insurance at all. And if you currently have a whole life policy, make sure you keep it in place until you fully replace it with term life. You never want to be without some form of life insurance.

collision and comprehensive coverage no matter what year your car is. This is because without it you would lose your car due to the accident and you wouldn't have any money to replace it. These are things that you and your agent will need to discuss in order to get you the best price.

Another huge money saver when it comes to insurance is your deductible amount. The higher your deductible the less money you will pay in premiums. For example, since you have at least $1000 in your emergency fund, you can set your deductibles to $1000 and save hundreds per year in premiums. I would definitely recommend this for your auto insurance and home owners insurance, at the very least. Your savings will be worth making the change.

The main thing to remember in the area of insurance is to use an independent agent to do the shopping for you and get you the best deals, make sure you have only the policies that you need, and make sure that your deductibles are as high as you can support in order to save the most money.

CABLE, INTERNET, AND CELL PHONES

When it comes to finding service in these areas, there are many companies out there to choose from. And this is good news for you – the consumer. This means that you have choices about who you want to give your business to and you get to make the decision based on service and price. When it comes to pricing, you almost always get the best pricing when you are willing to sign a contract. Don't look at this as a bad thing. It is good for them because they know that you will stay with them for a certain amount of time and good for you because you get a great deal for your loyalty. You can also save money by bundling products with some companies. I got a super deal a couple of years ago on my internet, cable and home phone. Just by shopping around and taking advantage of a deal that a company was offering with a 2 year signed contract, I received the lowest price I have ever seen with this bundle. Now, my contract is coming up in a month and I will begin shopping again. I hope that I can make a great deal with the same company, but I am willing to change if the price and service is better with someone else. This is where knowledge is power. Knowing what all of the companies are offering, you can use it to wheel and deal with the company you want to use and hopefully get them to match that price.

What is most important in every area is that you take the time to find out every single one of your options –

what is being offered and at what price. Never pay higher prices just because you don't want to take the time to research your options. You could be missing out on something great. Also, make sure you only have services that you need and are using. A great example of this is in the area of cell phones. Make sure that you only have the services that you are using on your plan and make sure that you are getting the best deal possible. If you text a lot, don't pay per text – get an unlimited texting plan. If you have a data plan, make sure that you can use data on your phone and then monitor your usage. Don't pay for more than you need. I have worked with people who had trouble paying their bills, but their cell phone bill was $400. Work on getting this bill and all of your other utility bills as low as you can. And if it is still more than you can afford, you may have to drop something that is a luxury and not necessary. Hopefully you will be able to keep the luxury at an affordable price and the best way to do this is to shop it.

There are also some items and utilities that cannot be shopped because they are set by the company and you do not have a choice in which company you use. For items like this, however, you can set up a budget plan which will make the payment the same every month no matter what you usage is. An example of this would be your electric bill. Basically they take your usage for the last year and average it out over twelve months of bills. If you go over or use less than this amount at the end of the year, they adjust your bill accordingly for the next year. This is a great plan to get on if it is offered, not because it saves you money, but because it helps you when doing your budget and helps you to keep it consistent throughout the year. Your goal is to make your budget as low and as consistent as possible and hopefully the information in this chapter will help you to reach that goal and move on to wealth and financial freedom.

SUMMING UP WEEK 12

This week has been all about getting the most for your money. This is not only something that you need to do right now, but something that you will always do, even as a wealthy person. Wealthy people don't just do some magic program until they become wealthy and then stop. It is all about lifestyle and a new way of thinking. When you are getting the most for your money, you are protecting your wealth.

This week I want you to shop around in the areas that we discussed and make sure that you are getting the most for your money and see if there are any changes you can make that will save you money. In the area of insurance, contact your local independent insurance agent (if you live in VA, SC, PA, NJ, MD, or DE, you can contact my agent, Tom Davenport, of Blue Marsh Insurance at 877-MARSH80). They should be able to get you quotes on the best coverage and the lowest price in all areas – auto, life, long term disability and health. When it comes to the other areas we discussed – cable, internet and cell phones – you need to call around to the companies that are offered in your area and find out what deals they can give you for the services that you want. I recommend that you go into the cell phone carrier stores (the actual carrier stores, not the guys who sell every carrier) and talk to a salesperson in person to find out what kind of deal you can get with them. If you currently have a carrier, you may not be able to change carriers until your contract is up without a fee, but it is great to have the information and be armed with the knowledge so that you know what is out there for when it is time.

The last thing you need to check on is if your utility companies, such as electric or gas, offer a budget program that you can sign up for. This will keep your payments even and easier to manage throughout the year.

This week has been all about saving money and getting the most for your money. If you never shop around, whether it is for things or for services, you could be throwing precious money away – money that could be invested and make you a lot more money. This is the reason that this week is so important in your wealth journey. You want to be able to have what you want, but you want to get it at a price that you can afford and at a price where you have money left over to invest and build your wealth. The end result of getting the biggest bang for your buck is wealth and financial freedom. On to week 13!

WEEK 13

TAKING STOCK OF YOUR LIFE

Do you feel happy all of the time? Do you have joy in your life even when things aren't going exactly as you had planned? Wealthy people tend to be happy people, but not for the reason that you think. They are not happy because they have money and therefore, they have no problems. Wealthy people have just as many problems as you do – life happens to them the same as it happens to broke people. Wealthy people get cancer, wealthy people's cars break down, wealthy people lose loved ones, and wealthy people have bad days at work. What wealthy people have that most broke people don't have, however, is a positive attitude. They do not let people or situations steal their joy. They know that life happens and whatever their reality is, they can deal with it, fight it if they have to and move on. Wealthy people have hope and joy where broke people have misery and disbelief. That hope and joy is what brings positive situations into wealthy people's lives and eventually money.

How many times have you said "I'll be happy when..."? And then the "when" happens and you still aren't happy? You say "I'll be happy when I get a bigger house". Then you get the bigger house and your mortgage, taxes, insurance and utilities bills are bigger and now you seem to have less time on your hands because you have to clean the bigger house. Or you say "I'll be happy when I get that promotion". You get the promotion which involves more hours, dealing with difficult people and more responsibility. Therefore, the promotion didn't make you happier. The reason that these things still aren't making you happy is simple – your happiness doesn't come from things or situations, it comes from inside.

Did you know that you can choose to be happy every day? Did you know you can have joy even while you are sitting in traffic or while you are sitting on the side of the road waiting for a tow truck? Your happiness is in your hands and is what you think. This is why wealthy people tend to be happy people. It is not the money that made them wealthy; it is the attitude that made them the money. If you are not happy broke, you will not be happy wealthy. Money does not buy happiness. It may buy you a temporary moment of happiness, a rush if you will, but it doesn't buy true happiness.

If you own your own business, but you are not a happy person, your business won't do very well. However, if you own a business, and you are friendly and compassionate and truly believe that the customer is always right, your business will succeed. If you work in an office, but you are not a happy person, you won't go very far. However, if you work in an office, and you are easy to get along with, have ideas, take criticism well and work well with people, you will move up in the company. Being a happy, satisfied person will bring money your way without much effort. Do what you love and the money will follow.

This week I want us to look at the seven areas of your life that we talked about with goal setting and discuss some positive ideas for having success and happiness in each area. I am going to share some ideas and give you some examples, but you need to decide ultimately what each area should look like for you and then, next week, when we set our short and long term goals, you will have a better idea of which road to take and what changes are needed to get you happy and satisfied.

Career – This is the most important area when it comes to money simply because this is how you make your money. Without a career, you will never have money. And the best way to guarantee the most money is a career in something that you are passionate about. So many people go every day to a j-o-b with the sole purpose of bringing home enough money to pay the bills. If that is your attitude, that is all you will ever do – bring home just enough to pay your bills. You will never be wealthy because you don't think like a wealthy person. You are living day to day – paycheck to paycheck. You need to be doing something that you love to do. In today's world, you can find a way to make money doing almost anything you enjoy doing. I know people who have taken their hobbies and turned them into very successful businesses. You just need the determination and the know-how. The know-how is easier than you think – there are a lot of mentors out there, as well as books, blogs, etc. that you can read to learn what it takes to have a successful business in this society. But the determination is all on you. If you decide that you want to be successful, let nothing stand in your way. If you make a mistake or fail at something, learn from it and move on. Many of the best lessons we get come from mistakes. This is true whether you are trying to move up in a company or running your own business. Remember this – wealth isn't just about how much money you make. Wealth will come if you are doing something that you are passionate about and you go to work every day and do what you love to do. Don't settle for a j-o-b. Find your passion and do what you love every single day and you will have success.

Family and Friends – This is an area that can be a huge obstacle to wealth if you are not careful. Keeping up with the Joneses is one of the most common reasons that people spend more than they make. They are always trying to keep up with their friends and family and trying to live the life that they seem to be living. The reason that I said "seem to be living" is because there is a good chance that what you see isn't their reality at all. Many people who look like they have everything are up to their eyeballs in debt and are as broke as the day is long. All you need to do is be yourself and not worry about what everyone else has or is doing with their life. We are all unique – we have unique gifts and desires. And this is an awesome thing. You need to live the life that you want to live and stop worrying about everyone else. It will be challenging when you are driving around in a 10 year old car and your sister is driving a brand new car. It will be challenging when you go out to eat once a month and your friends go out one or two times a week. But in the long run, you have to live your life. If you owe $20,000 for a new car, is your sister going to help you pay for it? If you go into credit card debt in order to eat out every week, are your friends going to chip in? No, of course not. We are each responsible for our own lives and the best thing you can do is live your life daily and make decisions like a wealthy person would and don't worry about what everyone else thinks. If you want to be wealthy, do what wealthy people do, not what broke people do. You can love your friends and family and hang out with them, but you don't have to impress or become them.

Marriage – Marriage is about teamwork – being on the same page about the big stuff like kids, religion, family and money. And when you are not on the same page, life can be very challenging. 52% of marriages end in divorce and over 80% of those are due to finances. When you are struggling with money and spending more than you make, you are just adding fuel to the fire. Wealthy people tend to have good marriages. Again, not because they have money and therefore have no problems, but because they aren't as stressed about money which helps them to calmly resolve conflicts with compromise. When you are worried about how you are going to pay your mortgage, you can't be bothered with trying to come up with a compromise over something like who is going to pick up the kids. When you are stressed out about money, everything is an issue – even the small stuff. People who are stressed out about money tend to carry that stress over to their spouses, their kids, their family and friends and even their jobs. When you are financially successful, you are able to keep your joy and bring joy to others. The love that you have for your spouse should be a priority over how much money you have. And when it is, the money will take care of itself because you will work together to make the best choices for both of you and your future.

Personal Growth – If you think, now that you have graduated high school or college, you are done with learning, think again. You need to continue to learn and gain knowledge for your entire life. And not just in your career, but in other areas as well. Reading this book is a great start – I try to read at least six non-fiction books a year in many different areas. You don't have to have just one hobby – you can learn a different trade or how-to every year. Learning is fun and can open your world bigger than any amount of money can. Don't keep yourself in a box – this may be why you are having trouble in the area of your money. You have to be able to think outside of the box and think beyond the life you are living now. You can do and be anything – but you have to go get it. It won't come to you. You will not become wealthy by sitting on your couch in your sweats and watching television (although there is a time and place for that). You have to get out there and learn. You never know what you will find – for example, you could be reading a book on gardening and read a pearl of wisdom that will help you with your kids. The possibilities are endless – you just have to go after them.

Spiritual – If you are a person of faith, this is extremely important. The Bible is full of instructions about joy and happiness and about money. The thing that you need to keep in check is your love of money or your greed. If having money is so important to you that you will do anything to get it, there is an imbalance in your life. If you only spend money, but never give, there is an imbalance in your life. God wants us to have things – He loves to give us the desires of our heart and He also is the one who gave each and every one of us the ability to be wealthy (Deuteronomy 8:18). It is not God who is preventing you from becoming wealthy – it is you and the choices that you are making. Keeping in touch with God on a daily basis will help you more than you can ever know. God designed money as a means to an end. You need money to live, but you don't need to live for your money. And this applies, even if you are not a person of faith. We have seen over the last decade what happens when greed takes over our lives. Your goal should not be to see how much money you can accumulate at any expense; your goal should be to live a great life, making wise decisions, and the money will follow. This is why we all have the ability to be wealthy – no matter what our income is.

Physical Health – Obviously how healthy you are has a direct effect on your finances. The healthy you are the less your medical costs are going to be – from how many times you go to the doctor to the number of illnesses you end up with to the cost of your health insurance. Right now, we have a health crisis in our country. And the problem is not what you think. The main problem is how unhealthy most Americans are – and this epidemic causes a rise in health care costs. The best way to solve the health care "crisis" is not by passing laws, but by people getting healthier. Find something that you enjoy that gives you some form of exercise and do it at least 3 times a week - mine is Zumba, my sister's is running. But it can be anything. Instead of gossiping around the lunch table at work about how bad the health care system is, go out and walk. Instead of having a heated debate on Facebook about the system, go outside and walk around. Don't be a complainer – be a solver. Be someone who sees a problem and does what they can do to solve the problem. Do everything you can to keep your health care costs down and the result will be happiness and success, not only in your pocketbook, but also in you.

Financial – The best way to have success and happiness in your finances is to have a balance with your money – work, spend, save and give. You have to work – make sure it is something that you love doing. And with what you earn from working, spend some (80%), give some (10%) and save some (10%). With this "secret" formula – 80-10-10 – you will always have money. You will never find a wealthy person who is unbalanced in their financial world. Most wealthy people actually use more of a 60-20-20 formula. And this is because they want to do more than just have money – they want to be financially free and to help those less fortunate than they are. Yes, you will find stingy wealthy people. There are people who have millions and never give a dime. But this is rare and very uncharacteristic of the wealthy – especially first generation wealthy. As we said before, money will not buy you happiness, but it will afford you freedoms that broke people just don't have. And with these freedoms comes happiness and success.

Have you ever thought that you may be what is standing in your way from being wealthy? It is not someone else's job to make you happy and satisfied. That is your job and yours alone. If you marry someone just so they can make you happy all the time, you will be divorced in a few years. If you take a job, just for the money, hoping that the money will make you happy, you will quit within a few months. This week, you need to write out how you are happy and satisfied already in each of the seven areas and then write down what you can change to bring about the change you want to see in your life. You are the author of your story – no one else. Write down what needs to change to make your story a best seller.

SUMMING UP WEEK 13

Sometimes it is a good thing to take a few minutes and take stock of your life. That is what this week is about

– with a focus on happiness and satisfaction. If you are always going after the next big thing, you won't have time to enjoy the here and now and everything that it has to offer. Happiness does not come from things and money – it comes from a healthy balance in all areas of your life. This week you are going to address these areas – past, present and future – and see what changes you can make to find true happiness and satisfaction. You don't want the happiness of fairy tales; you want the happiness of a balanced, well rounded life full of joy and satisfaction with a little wealth and financial freedom on the side. On to week 14!

WEEK 14

SETTING SPECIFIC SHORT AND LONG TERM GOALS

This chapter may feel like déjà vu, but it isn't. The very first week, you set up your 3 year goals as a beginning in order to get an idea of which direction you wanted to head in seven areas of your life. This week, we are going to get very specific and set up both short and long term goals. It is imperative that you have goals for now and for the distant future and everything in between. If the only goals you have are for 3 years from now, you will miss out on many dreams and opportunities in between and beyond.

As a point of review, all goals need to have four components – they need to be written, be realistic, be specific and be adjustable. You need to dream big and go for whatever it is that you want to make happen and your goals need to reflect that. This week you are going to come up with goals for 6 months from now, 1 year from now, 5 years from now and 10 years from now. The goals should be bigger and better as time goes on. For example, your 6 month goal may be prepare yourself to open your own business – learn marketing, bookkeeping, social media, etc. Your 1 year goal may be to open that business at a certain location. Then, your 5 year goal may be to have $500,000 in sales and 20 employees and lastly, your 10 year goal may be to have $1 million in sales and 50 employees and 2 locations. All of these goals are written, they are realistic and obtainable, they are specific, and they are adjustable (you can up them as you go along).

I can't say this enough – goals are a vital tool when it comes to building wealth and becoming financially free. You can't just decide one day to be wealthy and hope that it happens somehow. You have to have a plan – something to guide you and something to aim for. It is also very important that you have goals both for now and in the future. Wealthy people don't just live in the moment – when they make a money decision today, they think about how it will affect them in a few months and a few years. Living day to day is the equivalent of living paycheck to paycheck. And living with a vision for the future is the equivalent of living wealthy.

As always, I will give you a few examples from each of the seven areas, but your goals are your own – not someone else's goals. Don't write down what your mom or dad want you to do or what Aunt Susie thinks you should do – write down what you want to do and where you see yourself in 6 months, 1 year, 5 years, and 10 years.

✯✯

10-10-10

In the book, "10-10-10", Suzy Welch has showed the effectiveness in decisions large and small, routine and radical, getting us out of neutral at home, in love, and at work by asking the question, "How will this decision affect you in 10 minutes, 10 months and 10 years?" This is how wealthy people think. Wealthy people always think beyond the moment. They think into the future and make the best decisions they can knowing what they know. Try using this method the next time you have a decision to make and see if your future answer is different than your impulse answer would have been.

✯✯

Career – As always, this area can be life changing in so many ways, but especially when it comes to setting goals. If you love what you do, you will never work. This is because when you love what you do every day it doesn't seem like work even though you make money at it. Rachael Ray has 5 jobs going at one time and yet she said just today that it never feels like work to her. It is because she loves what she does and is working in her true calling. If she couldn't work with food, she would be miserable. And she has felt this way always, even before her fame. This isn't about becoming famous – fame and fortune aren't what make you happy – it is about truly loving what you do every minute and being lucky enough to get paid to do it. That is how I feel every day and I want the same for each and every one of you. For 15 years, I didn't enjoy my jobs because they were just that, jobs. But then I found my passion, my true calling and now I love what I do every day. It isn't work for me – it is what I love to do. What would you do if money were not an issue? That is what you need to make your career and the money will follow. As we talked about in the last chapter, you can make money doing just about anything. So take what you would do for free and find a way to make money at it. And then set your goals accordingly.

Family and Friends – This area can be tough to set goals for at times. But it is just as important in order to keep balance in your life. Think hard about your relationships with your family and friends and reflect on what is missing in those relationships. Or what may be toxic in those relationships. You want to make sure that the people in your life are going to build you up, not tear you down. You can't change people, but you can love them from a distance. Accept people for who they are and move on. Set your goals up with what is best for you, but in a loving and caring way toward your friends and family. If you want to be in the same place 6 months from now or where your friends and family are, then keep doing what you are doing. But if you want to go places and be more, set goals and set them big. Your goals should always include having healthy relationships and positive people in your life, people that will climb to the top with you, not keep you at the bottom.

Marriage – We talked about last week how wealthy people have good marriages. In order to keep your marriage fresh, you need goals like you are going to set this week. I recommend having separate goals as well as goals together in this area. As an individual, you should have goals regarding what you want to contribute to the marriage. And as a couple, you should have goals that can be done together to keep the marriage fresh and alive. You want to fall in love with your partner more every day, not grow more apart. And your goals should reflect this.

Personal Growth – If you are not growing, you are staying where you are. If you want to be more and have more, you need to do more. Don't just sit around waiting for your ship to come in or your lottery numbers to come up. Decide in what areas you want to grow and learn and set your goals accordingly. You also can have more than one goal per time frame. For example, you may set a goal to read 12 books over the next year and learn how to play the piano. When it comes to your personal growth, there should be no limits. Of course, don't do too much at once, but don't limit yourself to one thing per year either. You may never know if you like something until you try it – so try it. Don't sit around wishing – go and do it.

Spiritual – If you are a person of faith, your walk with God and your knowledge of the Bible is an ongoing thing. You never have everything you need in this area. Even if you have read the Bible through all the way, you still don't have everything you need. I have been a Christian since I was 10 and I grew up in church my entire life and I have learned more in the last 10 years than I ever did just going to church. And this learning should be reflected in your goal setting. Your only goal can't be just to go to church 1, 2 or 3 times a week. Church is good, but it is your daily walk and your thinking and your being that is most important. Your spiritual life is important whether you believe in God or not. We all have something on the inside of us that helps us to make right decision and do the right thing. Make sure that your goals reflect nurturing that in a positive way. Making good decisions and doing the right thing is an important step to wealth and financial freedom so set your goals accordingly.

Physical Health – Having wealth won't do you any good if you are not around to enjoy it. Whether you are 25 or 65, eating right and exercise are very important parts to a balanced life and longevity. This doesn't mean that you have to be a marathon runner or an Olympian; it just means that you need to move. A survey came out just this week that said that overweight people who exercise live three years longer than skinny people who don't. This also doesn't mean you can never have cake or ice cream; it just means everything in moderation. Do what you need to do and set your goals up in a way that keeps you on this earth as long as possible. That way you can enjoy the wealth and financial freedom that you worked so hard to reach.

Financial – Well, this should be an easy one. You are reading this book in order to have a financial life of wealth and financial freedom and your goals should reflect just that. Use everything that you are learning about how the wealthy make decisions and how they handle their money to set your goals for your money. This can include making good money habits goals, savings goals, getting out of debt goals, even goals about how you are going to buy your next car. Set up your financial goals to reflect a life of wealth and financial freedom.

Setting your goals is not just a one-time thing. You can't just set a 6 month goal, reach it and be done. If that were the case, after 10 years, you would have nothing to aim for anymore. You should set aside time each week to look over your goals and make sure they are still what you want and that you are on the right path to achieve them. If not, adjust them accordingly. And when you reach a goal, make sure to set a new one. Your goals should move with you and continue for as long as you are walking this earth. Even if you are in a nursing home, you should have goals. Never give up on having exactly what you want to have in life. It is your life and you are the author of your story.

SUMMING UP WEEK 14

You cannot simply decide to be wealthy and sit around waiting for it to happen. If it were that easy, everybody would be wealthy. One of the main characteristics of the wealthy is that they are goal oriented. They have goals in all areas of their life – both short term and long term goals – and they do everything they can to reach those goals. And if they can't or change their minds, they simply revamp the goal and keep going. They never give up on their goals and dreams. They press through, even when it is difficult. This week you will take one more step toward becoming the wealthy person you want to be. You will set 6 month, 1 year, 5 year and 10 year goals in all seven areas of your life. Remember, these goals need to be written, specific, realistic and adjustable. Goals are not only something that you are setting this week and then moving on. Goals must be a part of your life from now on. You need to always have something to aim for and a dream to reach. Goal setting is a necessary step to wealth and financial freedom. On to week 15!

WEEK 15

LEAVING A LEGACY

Your legacy is not just about how much money you leave behind. Your legacy encompasses everything that you leave behind. We have all lost someone very close to us and we all know how much pain grief can bring. We should be able to grief properly for our loved ones and not have to deal with difficult financial issues during this time. Unfortunately, many times this is not the case. And this is why leaving a great legacy is so important.

Leaving a money legacy has its place. We all want to build wealth and be able to pass that wealth on to our kids, grandkids, and beyond. But that legacy can come at a very big price if the recipients are not equipped to handle it. Part of leaving a legacy is leaving it in such a way that is going to benefit all parties concerned. Make sure if you are leaving a large amount of money behind that you check with an estate planning attorney to advise you on the best way to set up your estate, not only for tax purposes, but also for emotional purposes. You wouldn't hand an alcoholic a drink; don't hand a person who can't handle money well a bunch of money. It won't be good for them or for the legacy you are trying to leave. This is where the estate attorney can help you.

Just as important as the money legacy is the estate legacy. An estate is anything that you leave behind so you can have an estate even without being wealthy. Your estate not only consists of money and items, but also includes the essential paperwork needed in the event that something happens to you. And making sure that you have that paperwork is our main focus this week.

YOUR LEGACY

Everyone, no matter whether you have $1 or $1million, needs 3 legal documents: a will, a power of attorney and a living will. A will is needed in any and all situations. Most of us know that we need a will, but many people never get around to getting one, leaving the courts to decide who gets – or doesn't get – what. A will can be as simple or as complicated as you want it to be, but you must have one in place. If you leave no other legacy, leave this one. Otherwise, your family, who are already grieving, will be put through more pain by having to deal with the courts when they should be mourning their loss.

A power of attorney is an important document to have even while you are still here with us. This gives someone – a spouse, a child, a family friend – the right to speak for you anytime that you cannot speak for yourself. Do not assume that just because you are married that you do not need this document. There are many situations where even a spouse cannot speak for you without a power of attorney. You want to make sure that the person speaking for you has your best interests in mind and a court – who could make the decisions without a power of attorney – will not.

A living will is important for the same reasons as the other two documents. You always want your wishes to be played out and these three documents assure that this will be the case. A living will simply lets you decide what will happen to you in end-of-life and life support situations.

None of us ever want to think about dying and most of us avoid it unless we are forced to face a certain situation. But the reality is that no one knows when they will leave this earth and the best legacy that you can leave your family is the legacy of preparedness. These three forms are simple and don't cost much at all ($29 total for all three at www.uslegalforms.com at the time of publication). But they will be priceless to your family when your time comes.

What happens to my debt when I am gone?

This is a very confusing subject when someone passes, but the answer is pretty simple. No one inherits your debts when you die. If you have a joint debt with someone, such as a spouse, the debt is still valid as they are still alive. But any debt that you have that has your name only on it dies with you. In the event of your passing, your spouse or heir simply needs to send a copy of your death certificate to the company along with a certified letter stating that you passed away and the account should be closed. As their spouse or heir, you do not owe the money. However, the person's estate must stand good for the debt. For example, if your spouse had a credit card with a balance of $1000, you would have to use his/her assets (cash, car, retirement account, etc.) to pay off the debt. And if the person didn't have any assets to cover the debt, then nothing would be owed. Basically, each person is responsible only for the debt that has their name on it and their assets are to be used to pay for this debt until either the debt or the assets are gone. You do not inherit debt.

YOUR LEGACY BOOK

In a drawer in my desk, is a binder full of everything my husband or I will need in the event of death. This is called our "Legacy Book". In our family, as in many families, I am the bookkeeper. We always make financial decisions together, but I execute them by writing the checks or filing the paperwork. It is hard enough to keep all of the accounts, passwords and wishes in check while we are alive, but when we are grieving it is almost impossible. This is where the "Legacy Book" is vital. This can take on any form you want and be located anywhere you want it to be, but it is crucial to have. This way, your spouse and children know exactly how to keep the finances going and what they need to know and deal with. Below are just some of the important things to have in your "Legacy Book":

- ❖ All life insurance policies – numbers, name of company and amounts.

- ❖ All bank account information – bank and account numbers and any passwords needed. This also includes safety deposit box information and key location.

- ❖ All retirement account information – companies, account numbers and balances.

- A copy of your will – the original should be in your safety deposit box or in a lockbox.

- A copy of your power of attorney – same as above, the original should be kept in a safety deposit box or in a lockbox.

- All mortgage information – company, account number, and balance. The deed should be in your safety deposit box or lockbox.

- A list of all of your debts – company, account numbers, and balances.

- If you are over 65, social security information. The surviving spouse is allowed to collect the higher of the two amounts. Therefore you need the information on both of you in order to process that request.

- The name of your lawyer, accountant, financial advisor and the executor of your estate – this will help the beneficiaries to know who to contact about your estate and wishes.

- A list of all usernames and passwords for any computers, email and websites you may use. For example, I use our bank's website for online banking. I would need to list the website and the username and password for my spouse.

- ❖ A list of your funeral wishes and the deed to your burial plot, if you have purchased it already. You should discuss these wishes with your spouse and family, but it needs to be written down as well.

- ❖ Deeds to any other property (second home, boat, cars, etc.) you own – originals should be kept in a safety deposit box or lock box and a copy made for the file.

This is just a beginners list to get you started. As with anything else, you need to tailor it to your personal situation. The "Legacy Book" should contain within it any and everything that your spouse or family could possibly need in the event of your death. It is better to have too much information than not enough.

When you leave this lovely place, you leave behind your integrity, your character, your money, your things and your life. This is your legacy. And the best legacy that you can leave is a legacy of preparedness –

preparing your heirs to deal with your death. I know that talking about death is not pleasant, but it is being responsible to make sure that everyone knows what they need to know. There should be no surprises when you are gone and no mystery as to what your wishes were. This book is all about learning from the wealthy and having their affairs in order at all times is something that is important to wealthy people – and should be just as important to you. Preparing your legal papers and your legacy book is a step you can take now as you set off on your journey to wealth and financial freedom.

SUMMING UP WEEK 15

This week is all about getting your legal life in order and setting up the necessary forms and information to make sure that your wishes are always followed through. You need to set up a will, power of attorney and living will if you do not have these forms already. You can use a lawyer if you want to, but you can also use uslegalforms.com as I referenced before. Either way, make sure that you have all three legal forms immediately if you don't have them already. You also need to set up your legacy book. You can use any kind of system that you want or simply put things in folders and keep them all together in a safe place that both you and your spouse (or heir) knows. Make sure you put anything and everything in your legacy book that you think someone might need if you weren't around. Your goal is to make your passing as stress free as you possibly can make it. People will grieve, but you want to bring as much peace after you are gone as you did while you were here. On to week 16!

WEEK 16

WEEK OF THANKSGIVING

You may or may not be reading this in November, but this week isn't about the holiday where we eat too much and watch football and parades. That holiday is just a representation of an attitude that should be a part of our everyday lives. Instead of taking one day a year and being thankful for everything and everyone, it should be something that you do every day and it is a vital step to wealth.

Having a thankful attitude and being content go hand in hand and if you are not either one, it will be very difficult to reach wealth and financial freedom. Let me give you an example by using an illustration of how a parent feels. If you have a child who is never grateful or never says thank you when you do something or buy something for them, after a while you are going to stop doing and buying for them. However, if you have a child that is content with what they have and is very grateful when you buy or do something for them and always says thank you, you automatically want to do more for them without them ever asking you. This is how the universe or God, for the person of faith, works as well. If you aren't thankful for what you do have, why should you be given any more?

When you respect your money, realize how hard you work to get it and how blessed you are compared to some people, you have an attitude of thanksgiving and you are content. And when you are thankful and content, you are not always looking for that next "thing" to make you happy. This makes it easier to save and invest in order to build wealth. However, when you are not thankful and content, you are always looking for that "thing" that will finally make you happy and you end up spending all of your money, and then some, to find it.

This week is all about thanksgiving and contentment. I want you to be wealthy and I know you want to be wealthy as well and this is a critical step toward that goal. I stressed in the beginning of this book how each week is just as important as the next and that there would be times where you would be tempted to skip a week thinking that is wasn't important. This is probably one of those weeks. And one reason may be that you think that you are content and are a thankful person and you probably are on some level. But we are going to take this week to fine tune both of these so that discontentment and unthankfulness never get in your way to wealth and financial freedom.

GREED

"The love of money is the root of all evil." This is one of the most misquoted verses in the Bible. Most people think that money is the root of all evil and therefore, it is greedy just to want money. And that is simply not true. We all have the God given ability to be wealthy and that is what he wants for us. We should always strive to have more, but not to the point where it becomes an obsession. Greed is a result of this obsession. When all you think about is money and how much money you can have and how you will do anything and hurt anyone to get it, that is greed. And by the way, that means hurting yourself.

No one sets out to be greedy. If I asked any of you right now if you are a greedy person, not one of you would answer yes. But there is a small chance that a little greed has crept in and that attitude is what has helped to get you in the pickle that you are in.

Somewhere along the way you said, even subconsciously, that you wanted something even though you knew that it wasn't the right time to have it. And you proceeded to get that something no matter how much it hurt you financially. And if you are like me, you have done this over and over and over until you have woken up and found yourself with no money and in debt up to your eyeballs. But don't worry – greed is not something that you are born with. It is something that can be changed and that is what this week is about.

Entitlement is another form of greed that is creeping into our society more and more. This is one that got me without me even having a clue what it was. When I graduated college 20 years ago, I believed that I was supposed to be able to have everything that my parents had and the only way I could do that was with debt. What I didn't realize was that my parents had what they had through many years of hard work, wise money decisions and savings. I just assumed that you went to school, graduated, got a job, and started getting things like new cars, new clothes and new homes. I didn't realize, at that time, that it takes years of hard work and sacrifice to get those things.

And nowadays it is even worse than that. Kids from a very young age, as young as 2 or 3, believe that can have anything they want, no matter what. And our teenagers and young people demand everything that they want whether they have the money to pay for it or not. You are not entitled to a new home – you have to save and set you finances up in such a way that you can comfortably afford a new home. You are not entitled to a brand new car just because you have a driver's license or because you got a new job – you have to save to pay cash for it so the payment doesn't become a burden. You really aren't entitled to anything, but you can have everything as long as you have the money to pay for it. And when you try to get it before that time, you cause yourself serious grief and problems.

Greed and entitlement are attitudes that can creep in without you even realizing that they are there. And they are attitudes that can impede your journey to wealth and financial freedom. This is one of those times where you are going to need to be completely honest with yourself and identify if you have a greedy or entitlement attitude, even if just a little. And if you do, as I did, hopefully, by the end of this week, you will turn those attitudes into attitudes of thanksgiving and contentment and move forward in your journey.

THANKSGIVING

We have identified two very important negative attitudes that can creep in and get in the way of our wealth journey. And now it is time to replace them with an attitude that will carry you all the way to the top – an attitude of thanksgiving. No matter what your financial status is right now, you have more than someone else. There are many people just in this country alone that do not have a roof over their heads, running water, food to eat, clothes to wear, heat in the winter, etc. Sometimes, we tend to get so caught up in our problems that we don't realize this fact. I'll never forget the first time I realized that not everyone has running water in this country. I knew of other countries where clean water was an issue, but not here in the United States, right? Wrong. I was in my thirties and I was watching an episode of "Extreme Makeover – Home Edition" and the family lived in a house that was barely standing and did not have running water in the house. I couldn't believe it. It was at that time that I started really noticing how lucky I was and how very blessed I was even though I had money problems. What I also realized was that my money problems were different than the money problems of that family. My money problems had been brought on by me and my need to have everything at any cost. I made enough money to live, but I spent more than I made so that put me into debt. I had enough money to pay for my needs; what I didn't have was enough money to pay for my wants.

This realization began my journey of thankfulness and has moved me forward in ways I had only dreamed of before. I began to be thankful for everything – thankful that I woke up in the morning, thankful that I could walk, thankful that I had a job, thankful that my car started and when it didn't, thankful for the tow truck and the mechanic who fixed it. When you realize how blessed you really are, it humbles you and helps you to be content with the blessings you have and helps you to be patient and wise with your money and your money decisions. When you are thankful for your paycheck, you will respect it. When you are thankful for your car, you will take care of it.

As I am writing this book, we are only about six weeks from Black Friday. How many of you sit around on Thanksgiving morning and look through all of the sales papers and figure out all of the stuff you are going to buy – a lot of it just because it is on sale? I used to do this. Now, don't get me wrong. If you want to buy something, Black Friday is the perfect time. We have saved up all year and waited until Black Friday to buy things many a time because the prices are never lower than that weekend. But, how many things do you buy and then don't use or use just once and put in a closet? Discontentment causes us to just buy and buy – hoping to find that special thing that will make us happy. But when we are content and thankful for what we already have, we tend to buy only what we really want or need instead of buying for the sake of buying. And when we spend our money that way, we will always have money left over to save and invest instead of being broke trying to outspend our discontentment.

This week, take the time every day to write down all of the things that you are thankful for – even the things that most of the time we take for granted. You may not realize this, but your attitude is a huge predictor of how your life is going to turn out. People with a negative attitude have negative things happen to them and tend to be very unhappy, angry people. People with a positive attitude have negative things happen as well, but they keep their chin up and a smile on their face through it all. People with a thankful attitude and people who are content tend to have wealth and financial freedom. When you want to have what someone else has, you have to do what they did to get it.

Being content is not the same as settling. Being content means to be happy where you are at the same time that you are trying to reach the next level. Settling is giving up. For example, you need to be content in your one room apartment while you save up to buy your first house. And if all you can afford is a small house at first, be content there until you save up enough to move up in house. Never say "I'll never be able to afford a house." That is settling and never reaching your dreams and goals.

Wealthy people never settle, but they know how to be content while they are waiting for the things that they want. Wealthy people also buy items with an attitude of longevity. This attitude is very helpful when it comes to contentment. When you buy items that will last, you aren't looking to replace them when the next thing comes along. Study the habits of the wealthy and you will see that they practice an attitude of thanksgiving and contentment every day. These attitudes help them to enjoy life and not chase the next big "thing". Learn to be thankful and content and the result will be wealth and financial freedom.

SUMMING UP WEEK 16

Be thankful on purpose – form a habit of being thankful every day for what you have. Everything that you have is a blessing and it needs to be treated as such. This week you need to focus on this list and write down everything that you can think of that you are thankful for. And as the weeks, months, and years go by, make sure that you keep adding to the list and refer to it every day. Never go out into the world without being thankful for at least one thing. When you have an attitude of thanksgiving and contentment, wealth and financial freedom will come naturally as a result. On to week 17!

WEEK 17

FAMILY WEEK

Wealthy people overall have longer lasting marriages, more successful kids and better family relationships than broke people. But just like before, it is not because they have money, therefore, they don't have any problems. Money is a result of a positive attitude and balanced lifestyle and wealthy people tend to be very balanced when it comes to family. When I decided that I didn't want to be broke anymore and I started researching how wealthy people thought and acted, I read a great book by Dr. Thomas Stanley entitled "The Millionaire Mind". Dr. Stanley spent years surveying and researching millionaires to find out what qualities they had in common and to find out what millionaires did differently from broke people.

You see, contrary to popular belief, wealth is not luck of the draw – it is not something that is decided when you are born. It is a result of a balanced lifestyle and wise decisions, both financially and otherwise.

Therefore, Dr. Stanley wanted to find out what those lifestyles and decisions looked like in order to help people like me who realized that wealth is a choice, not an inherited trait. One of the many things that he found out is that the typical millionaire couple has been married at least 28 years. And when it comes to family, it was said that "our lifestyles are congruent with strengthening relationships with friends and family, and many of our activities are not substitutes for wealth building but complements to it." In other words, strong family relationships helped them to obtain the wealth that they have.

This week is all about family. One of the obstacles preventing you from obtaining the wealth and financial freedom that you desire might be the relationships you have with your family – spouse, kids, and relatives. Sometimes we look at family as just our relatives; we tend to take our spouse's and kid's roles in our lives for granted. But this week we are going to work on all of these family relationships.

MARRIAGE

We are starting with marriage because if you are married, there is no relationship more important than the one you have with your spouse. This relationship can make or break your wealth journey. Spouses must work together when it comes to money and even though you don't have to have the same opinion about certain things, you do have to be in agreement. For example, if one of you believes in debt and that debt is how you will pay for things and the other one is opposed to debt, you are going to always have a problem. If both of you agree to use debt or both of you agree that debt will never be an option, you will have less of a problem in this area. In individual circumstances you can learn the art of compromise, but in general theory, you need to be on the same page. And if you are not, you are always going to be stressed about money and money will be the cause of many fights in your relationship.

You see, if you both discuss a situation and come to a mutual answer and something goes wrong, you will work together to get out of it. But if only one of you decides and something goes wrong, then that person will be blamed and feel guilty about their mistake. It is imperative that you both, as a couple, be on the same page when it comes to money. I am a firm believer that couples should have joint accounts for everything, but I have met couples that have a joint account for household things and separate accounts for each of them for their individual stuff. Now, even though this isn't something that I would do, it works for them and they are in agreement so they will not have fights regarding this issue like someone would if one spouse wanted joint accounts and one spouse wanted separate accounts. This setup would cause friction and would have one spouse feeling like the other spouse didn't trust them.

80 – 90% of all marriage counseling sessions have money disagreements as the main reason that the two parties are there. Because whatever issues you have as an individual and as a couple always shows its ugly head when the subject of finances comes up. Each person in a marriage just wants to be loved, respected and have their voice heard. When you are on the same page when it comes to your finances, these actions are a natural result. And these actions result in wealth and financial freedom because you won't be spending

your time worrying and fighting over money; you will be spending your time making money and building wealth.

But when one or both of the parties doesn't feel loved and respected or that their voice is being heard, your time will be spent fighting. And let me just throw in here that if someone is feeling that way, it is valid whether the other person sees it or not. This is where communication becomes vital to a marriage. I am a strong believer in communication in all areas of your life – people can't read your minds. But in the area of marriage, it is extremely important. Make sure the other person knows how you feel and where you are coming from, not in an overbearing way, but in a loving way. Love is not a noun; it is a verb which means that it is an action word. Love is not something you feel; it is something that you act out every day.

Wealthy people have long lasting marriages because they get this concept and it shows throughout all areas of their lives including their money. As we have seen in other areas, for example goal setting, all of the areas of your life spill into each other. What happens in your marriage doesn't just affect your marriage; it affects every area of your life. This week, evaluate your marriage and decide what you need to change or to do in order to get balance. You can't change other people, only yourself, but you can decide to show them you love them and respect them and that their voice does matter. The Golden Rule is "do unto others as you would have them do unto you" not treat them the way they treat you. Show your spouse how you want to be treated by treating them that way. A healthy marriage is a factor in building wealth and financial freedom and brings with it the joy of having someone you can love and who loves you every minute of every day. Who wouldn't want that?

KIDS

We are raising adults – not kids. From the time our kids are born, we begin teaching them all of the things that they need to know, whether we realize it or not. Whether you teach your kids with words, actions or both, you are teaching your kids and molding them into the adults that they will become. This is why your relationship with your children is so important. We, as parents, want only the best for our children. I have never once heard a parent say "I hope my child has trouble." As a matter of fact, it is in trying to give them the best and help them to be the best that sometimes we make our biggest mistakes because we tend to smother them and give them everything they want, assuming that it makes their life easier.

And nothing could be further from the truth. I learned this about my relationship with my parents later on in my life. As I was growing up, I thought my parents were strict with too many rules and to some extent they may have been. They tried to protect me and they expected me to make the right decisions all of the time so that I didn't get hurt. But it was those mistakes that made me a stronger person. Bailing me out of the things I got myself into was their way of loving me, but in fact, they were not helping me. I needed to have consequences for my mistakes. And finally one time, when I was older, I did. And that experience changed my life forever. It hurt my parents to watch me go through it, but it was the best thing that could have ever happened to me.

This teaching has to start early, when the decisions and consequences are smaller. A great example is in the area of money. Teach your kids to spend, save and give a portion of their allowance every time you pay them. When it comes to spending, talk them through the process of making the best decision, but realize that the final decision has to be theirs. And when they regret that decision, talk them through it and help them see what would have been a better way. But don't bail them out. My daughter is a teenager and is at the age of wanting everything. She has to buy what she wants with her own spending money and at this age she wants everything. When she is talking about buying something, I usually talk through with her how much she really wants the item and what its purpose will be and whether or not I think she should get it. But the ultimate decision is hers. And she has a closet full of bad decisions. However, they are getting less and less because she is learning from her mistakes.

Our kids have to learn how to make decisions and how there are consequences, both good and bad, that come with those decisions. This is a part of raising adults. Wealthy people do the same thing with their kids. Just because they have money, doesn't mean that they go around buying them everything that they ask for. Wealthy people know the importance for being there for their kids and teaching them instead of telling them. If you are not doing this or you feel some sort of distance when it comes to your kids, work this week on the steps that you can take to spend more time with your kids and help them to learn to navigate this wonderful thing we call life.

The biggest money lesson that your kids need to learn is that work equals money. So set up some kind of plan for them to earn their allowance – don't just hand it to them. Have a balance between doing things because they are a part of the family (no money) and doing things to earn their allowance. This will teach them the most important lesson when it comes to money and building wealth.

Having positive healthy relationships with your family, whether it is your spouse, your kids or your relatives is an element to the process of building wealth. When you have those healthy relationships, you will be in a better frame of mind and make better decisions, not only with money, but with life. Making those positive decisions will lead you to the life of wealth and financial freedom that you want to have.

SUMMING UP WEEK 17

This week is all about family. I want you to take the entire week and focus on your family. And sometime during the week, take a look at the individual relationships with your spouse, you kids and your relatives. Figure out if you have that family balance that is important and if not, figure out what you need to do to get it. It is never too late to change directions, if need be, and move in the direction that not only will bring you joy and happiness, but the direction that will also bring you wealth and financial freedom. On to week 18!

WEEK 18

"THE MILLIONAIRE MIND"

In the introduction of this book, I talked about how being wealthy can mean different things to different people. For a lot of people it is a magic number - $1 million; most people would never even consider themselves wealthy unless they were worth at least a million. But being a true millionaire – or wealthy person – is about more than just how much money you have or what you own. It is about how you got there. You see, we all have the ability to be wealthy, but many people fall short of this potential.

If you ever take the time to study wealthy people – and I have – you will find that they have very similar characteristics, goals, dreams, and thinking. It is not that they are better than anyone else, but they have a certain way of looking at life and dealing with situations that has put them in the position that they are in – both in life and in money. The good news is that these characteristics are not born; they are made. This means that no matter what has happened in your past, you can change a few things right now and completely change the direction of your life. That is what this book is all about. But you have to be willing to make those changes. Wealth isn't about luck; it is about decisions.

When you get knocked down, do you get back up and keep going or do you stay down and make sure everyone hears about it? When someone puts you down or says something negative about you, do you get offended and mad and let what they said affect your life or do you believe in yourself and know who you are no matter what other people say or think? Do you look at the good in other people and in situations or are you always negative? How you answer these questions can determine whether or not you will be wealthy.

When you want to learn something, you need to learn from the best. Therefore, if you want to learn to be wealthy, you need to learn from other wealthy people. This week is all about delving into the mind of the wealthy and seeing what their characteristics, goals, dreams and thinking are in the seven areas of life that we have been using. In studying this, you should be able to see areas where your thinking and actions may be different and where you should make some changes in order to be able to succeed in your wealth journey.

What we are going to learn this week is not just based on one millionaire. It is based on surveys and studies done on thousands of millionaires all over this country. And these are not people who inherited their money – a few, yes – but it is people who succeeded based on wisdom, common sense, and sheer determination. And about the few who did inherit it – they wouldn't still be millionaires if they didn't have some of these characteristics. Money simply highlights what is already there – good or bad.

"THE MILLIONAIRE NEXT DOOR"

There are many more millionaires in this country than you may ever know. There are 3 kinds of millionaires: the obvious millionaires, the fake millionaires, and the millionaires next door. The obvious millionaires are just that – obvious. You can see their success and you know for a fact that they are millionaires. Then there are the fake millionaires. These are the people who give the illusion of being millionaires, but their actual net worth is very low. In other words, they may live in a million dollar home, but it has an $800,000 mortgage on it. That means their net worth is only $200,000, not one million. And last there are the millionaires next door. These are the people who have a net worth of a million dollars, but you would never know it by how they live. They don't drive fancy cars or live in big houses. They live middle class lives with upper class thinking.

The biggest thing to take away from this is to be careful who you mimic when learning to be wealthy. The best people to mimic are the millionaires next door, but it is challenging since you are not always sure who they are. Next would be the obvious millionaires. But I would caution you about ever taking advice from the fake millionaires. Their world is an illusion and that is the last thing you need.

This week we are going to learn about the characteristics, dreams, goals and thinking mostly of the millionaire next door with a little obvious millionaire thrown in. Pay very close attention to the information included in the next section. If you really take it to heart and stay determined, it will change your life forever.

ACTING AND THINKING LIKE A MILLIONAIRE

As we have discussed, true millionaires and wealthy people have very distinct thinking and characteristics that have helped them get to where they are today. This is where you want to be; therefore, let's dive right in and see what we can see.

Career – When it comes to career, 32% of millionaires own their own businesses, 16% are corporate executives, 10% are attorneys and another 10% are physicians. The rest encompass many different titles from retirees to teachers. What this shows us is that it is not always about how much you make, but what you do with it. We know this by this simple fact: $100 a month invested in good growth stock mutual funds from age 25 – age 65 yields you around $1.7 million.

So if the income isn't as important as the outgo, then why is your career so important to becoming wealthy? One word – passion. If you love what you do every day, you can't help but be successful and make money. That is why so many millionaires are self-employed. When they couldn't find what they wanted to do out in the job market, they made their own job instead of settling.

Another common characteristic when it comes to the careers of millionaires is being a leader and serving others. The best way for you to be successful is to help others reach their goals and dreams. Believe in people, help people, don't judge them and you will change their lives and in return, enrich yours. Wealthy people are not selfish dictators. They are loving people who honestly care about other people and put them first, not themselves.

Family – Family is very important to the wealthy. Wealthy people are not only kind and loving to the people in the work place, but also in their families. Even if they don't agree with something that a family member does, they don't judge them or stop speaking to them. They love them the best and most healthy way they can. Having healthy family relationships is important because it plays a big role in your thinking and your attitude. If you haven't had good family relationships up to this point, you know what I mean. There can be a lot of anger, regret, "why me", and blame. But the great news is that your past doesn't affect your future. No matter how you were raised or how your family treated you, your future can be different. Your family may include many people or just one; either way, make sure your relationships are loving and healthy. You are not in control of how other people act, but you are in control of you. Sometimes this means forgiving someone even if something seems unforgivable. Sometimes this means being the bigger person and saying you are sorry even if you didn't start it. Whether you are a family of one or of many, whether your family is blood or not, make the most of the relationships, show compassion, forgiveness and love and know when to love from a distance.

Marriage – Wealthy people say that the relationship that they have with their spouse is the most important relationship they have. There is a correlation between healthy marriages and wealth. This doesn't mean if you are divorced, you can't be wealthy. But if you are married, having the support of your spouse and being on the same page with your spouse is very important. You can have different opinions and you should, but as we talked about earlier, being on the same page is vital. When millionaires are interviewed, they credit much of their success and wealth to the relationship they have with their spouse. You can't make positive decisions and wise financial choices if you are fighting all of the time and you have a stressful marriage. Having a supportive spouse and a spouse, who gets you and loves you anyway and is always on your team, even when you don't agree, is very important in the wealth journey.

Personal Growth – Were you ever told in school that you just weren't college material? Or were you ever called just average? One of the things we know most about millionaires is that many of them do not even have a college degree and that many were told they were just average. I think that this is because doing well with money is mostly common sense, not book learning. If you have passion about something and use common sense, you can do just about anything, whether you got a 600 on your SAT's or a 1600. Wealthy people are always trying to educate themselves, long after the age of 21, by learning new skills, reading lots of books, and keeping themselves well informed and educated. You do not need a college education to be wealthy; you simply need a desire to continue gaining knowledge no matter how old or how wealthy you become.

Spiritual – When surveyed, millionaires ranked a relationship with God near the top as a reason for their wealth. This doesn't mean that only Christians can be wealthy. This just shows the correlation between faith and wealth. When people are at peace and feel that they have someone larger than themselves to turn to, it helps them to make better money decisions. Also, as a person of faith, they have studied the best book ever written on how to handle money – the Bible. There is also a lot to be said about having a close church family and being involved within a church. I know many people who feel as close to their church family as they do their own family. Like I said, you don't have to be a person of faith to be a millionaire, but believing in something beyond just ourselves is a great stepping stone to wealth and financial freedom.

Physical Health – One of the surveys I read said that most millionaires exercise in some form or another. My first thought was "Uh oh, I'm in trouble." But then I realized why exercise was so important. Being a person who has struggled with her weight, I know how being overweight at times can make you feel lethargic and drained of all energy. When you feel like this, you don't always feel like doing what you need to do every day. When you feel like this, you tend to not pay attention to the things that are important in the area of money, like budgets and investing. Exercise, even just a little every week, keeps your brain and your body energized. Exercise puts a little pep in your step and keeps you going for all of the things that you need to do. How you treat your body will determine how long you live and you want to be around long enough to enjoy what you have worked so hard to gain.

Financial – This seems obvious, doesn't it? Wealthy people are good with their money and that is why they have money. But what are they doing with their finances that you are not doing with yours? The first thing is wealthy people have a great respect for their money. They realize how hard they had to work to get it and how quickly it can go away if not respected. Wealthy people always spend less than they make. They never buy anything that they don't have the money to buy and they never pay more for an item than it is worth. Wealthy people give first, invest in their future second, and spend last. And they look beyond today, into the future and plan for it. Wealthy people are a group of fixers, not replacers. Millionaires have money for one reason and one reason only; they didn't spend it all. And what they didn't spend, they invested in their future. You cannot live moment to moment and day to day and be a millionaire. You have to live for the future.

I hope you enjoyed your trip into the millionaire mind. I know when I took my trip 15 years ago, it was very eye opening for me and I hope it has been the same for you. I cannot say this enough – becoming a millionaire is not about luck or chance or fate. It is about being the person that you were put here to be, doing everything with a positive attitude and with positive thinking and respecting the money you have. I hope after this week you have a better understanding of how a millionaire becomes a millionaire and that this will help you on your road to wealth and financial freedom.

SUMMING UP WEEK 18

This week has been all about learning from millionaires what it takes to become wealthy. When you want to become a scientist, you study other scientist and learn from them and the same is true about wealthy people. And remember, this information comes straight from the millionaires themselves. I hope that you have seen a few areas where you can make some positive changes in order to succeed in your journey to wealth and financial freedom. And I hope that you will make those changes so that you too can have a millionaire mind. On to week 19!

WEEK 19

STAYING IN BOUNDS

Boundaries are an important part of our everyday lives. There are boundaries that other people set for us and boundaries that we set up for ourselves. Within both types, there are boundaries that we are very aware of and some that we are not. But no matter what kind or how much awareness we have, boundaries are an essential element to wealth.

Can you imagine watching a football game being played with no boundaries? The players wouldn't know where to go and where to stop and there would be no marks of success, i.e. the end zone. Can you imagine driving down the road with no boundaries? Well, let's not even go there. Let's just say you wouldn't get very far. And that is how it is when it comes to boundaries in your life and in your finances.

This week we are going to focus on the boundaries that are already set up and the boundaries that you need to set up when it comes to your finances. I hope that during this week you will see the importance of having boundaries and that you will explore this concept in all of the other areas of your life as well, not just your finances. But right now, let's just focus on the money and how boundaries in this area, if followed and set correctly, can lead to wealth and financial freedom.

PRESET BOUNDARIES

There are many boundaries in our lives that are preset, meaning that we have no control over them. We can ignore them and slip over them, but they are there whether we like it or not. The lines on a road, the laws of the land, and the taxes we owe are just a few examples of boundaries in our lives that are preset. We have no control over where the lines are painted, setting the law, or the taxes that we owe out of our income. And many boundaries, like the first two, are boundaries that are designed to keep us safe and out of harm's way.

You do have control, however, over whether you respect the boundaries or not. And disrespecting them always comes at a cost. The great news for you is that most of the boundaries when it comes to your finances are set by you. There are some things that are preset, but within those presets, you have choices. For example, you do not have a say in the price of chicken, but you do have options in order to get the lowest price. Another example is you do not have a choice in the salary of your job, but you do have a choice in whether you accept it or move on. Yes, you can negotiate your salary and many other things, but there is only so far that you can go and then you have to make a choice. If you want it, you will accept it or you won't get it.

The great thing about your life is that it is yours and that you, and you alone, control it. You may not always be able to control everything when it comes to your money, but respecting what you can't control and controlling what you can control is a huge step to wealth and financial freedom. You may not be able to control the price of chicken, but you can control your menu and your list and your grocery budget in order to deal with the price of chicken. You may not be able to control your salary, but you can control your budget, your expenses and your work ethic in order to succeed within your boundaries and open yourself up for more. Focus on what you can control and respect what you can't.

PERSONAL BOUNDARIES

Personal boundaries are boundaries that you can control. Most of the boundaries in your life and in your finances are going to be personal boundaries – meaning that you will have complete control over how far you go. If you choose to have zero boundaries in your life, life will be more challenging for you. I have learned through everything that I have been through in my life that boundaries are essential. When I didn't have any or had very few, my life always ended up in a mess. Boundaries help you say "This is as far as I can go without bringing pain into my life."

In your finances, boundaries are a must. You will find that all wealthy people have many boundaries when it comes to their money. This is a major element that has contributed to their wealth and financial freedom. It would be really hard for me to list every boundary that you should have when it comes to your money and building wealth, and as with everything else in the area of your finances, boundaries are personal. However, I would love to share a few boundaries that have helped me in my wealth journey and are also shared by many others who have seen success in the area of their finances.

Your most important financial boundary is your income. You will never be wealthy spending more than you make. Therefore, your income is your boundary and if you go beyond that boundary, there is a price to be paid. That price comes in the form of debt, lack of savings and retirement, money stress and more. You must live below your means in order to have wealth.

And along those lines, another boundary needs to be never using debt to buy anything. Debt will never equal wealth – no matter how modern the math; therefore, do not buy anything based on money you may or may not have in the future. Nothing is guaranteed so never go outside the boundaries of your actual cash.

You also must have boundaries on your spending in order to stay within the boundary of your income. This is where budgets and spending journals come in very handy. Spending journals help you see where your money is actually going and budgets help you decide, within the boundary of your income, where your money needs to go.

Sometimes, when it comes to money, we have to set special boundaries for ourselves in order to protect us from the emotions of money. Remember, personal finance is 10% math, but is 90% emotions. One of the extra boundaries that I had to set for myself was in the area of the small stuff. It was easy to set boundaries on the big items: cable, phone, mortgage, groceries, etc. But sometimes I would look up and be $100 over budget and I couldn't figure out why. Finally, I realized it was the small stuff: a book, online gaming, household items, movies, etc. I didn't want to deprive myself of these things, so I set boundaries on those items as well.

I love to play a couple of games on my iPad in between writing and working, just to break up the day. But I learned that if you are not very careful, those games can end up costing you a lot of money to play. For example, Candy Crush Saga is one of the most popular games right now. It is free to play, but you can purchase things to help you along. I know people who have spent hundreds of dollars per month on just this one game alone. It is always okay to have fun and do what you enjoy, but be careful that you have boundaries so that you don't lose control.

Wealthy people have many boundaries – big and small. They live well, but they live wise. And wealthy people never throw their money away. You will find wealthy people who play the lottery or go to a casino, but it will be for entertainment purposes only, not as a solution to their money woes.

You may think that having boundaries in your life limits your life. It doesn't limit your life. A boundary is simply you looking at your situation and saying I can go this far and not get hurt. But if I go beyond this, I will experience pain and negative consequences. And also know that your boundaries will change as your financial situation changes. The more wealth you build, the wider your boundaries can be. For example, you may only be able to go out to eat once a month right now. But someday, you will be in a position to go out to eat once a week, if you want to. Boundaries bring wealth and financial freedom and boundaries keep you wealthy and financially free.

SUMMING UP WEEK 19

I hope I have helped you to see just how important having boundaries when it comes to your money really is. It is one of the key elements that turned my financial world around. It is a subject that isn't talked about much when you are talking about money. But it is vital.

Therefore, this week is all about you setting up boundaries in your finances. Remember, this is an ongoing process, as most of this book is, but I would bet that right now you have very few boundaries when it comes to your money. So start somewhere. And when something isn't working out in your finances the way that you want it to, check to see if a boundary is necessary to help you get to where you want to be. Just like the lines and guardrails on the side of the road are there to keep you save and protected, boundaries in your finances will keep you wealthy and financially free. On to week 20!

WEEK 20

GOOD VS. BAD

"If you make enough good habits, there won't be any room for the bad." Well, it has been a few months since you began the process to form new, good habits especially in the area of your finances. You made a list of all of the bad habits that were getting in the way of you winning in the area of money and you picked one habit to change from a negative to a positive. I hope that this process went well for you and you saw the success you hoped for in this area. I also hope that, even if you had trouble starting, that you didn't give up and now you have a great new money habit.

As the quote says in the beginning, the more good habits you form, the less room you will have in your life for bad habits. Wealthy people have bad habits, but they are a very small percentage of their life. Having a higher percentage of good habits will lead you toward a good life just like a high percentage of bad habits will lead you toward a less successful life. My guess is that up until now, you have leaned more toward the bad than the good when it comes to your money. I understand because that is exactly where I was. From day one, I formed some really bad money habits that stayed with me for many years. But learning that I could replace each and every one of them with a good money habit and turn my finances around changed my life. And it is never too late to start.

The key that I found to forming good habits was to focus on just that – forming the new habit. Don't focus as much on breaking the bad habit. It is all about replacement. Once you form a good habit, the bad habit will go away on its own. And don't forget, addictions are habits too. Any addiction can be overcome with the right guidance and lots of determination. Don't let anything stand in the way of the life that you want to have.

ONE MORE TIME

Since it has been a few months since you picked the first good habit that you wanted to form, I think that you are ready and strong enough to move on to the next good habit. I have dedicated a whole week to this decision and process because I know how hard it is and how important it is to the wealth building process. I also know how easily a bad habit can sneak back in when you least expect it to.

I have mostly good money habits at this point in my wealth journey. But even now, 15 years later, a bad habit will try to sneak back in if I am not careful. Forming good habits and defeating bad ones is an ongoing process, especially the longer you have had the bad habit.

When it comes to habits, you will have to dig deep in order to recognize all of the ones that are getting in the way. This is because so many times we accept things as "just the way they are" when the reality is that things are sometimes a bad habit that we have formed without ever knowing it. Everything that we do – our actions and our thoughts – are just habits that we have formed over our lifetime. This means that when something we are doing or thinking isn't working for us, we have the ability to change it. Believe in yourself today and know that you can have the exact life that you want and desire to have. All you have to do is take the necessary steps to make the changes that need to be made. This week focus on a bad habit – something that you are doing that is preventing you from becoming wealthy.

GOOD HABITS VS. BAD HABITS

I just wanted to take a minute to share some good habits and some bad habits to help you recognize some that you might not have thought of.

Good	Bad
Save 10% of your income	Spend 100% of your income
Use cash/debit card for purchases	Carry a balance on your cards
Do a written monthly budget	Spend until your $ runs out
Never impulse buy	Buy items without thinking
Buy a lottery ticket occasionally	Have a gambling addiction
Only go to the mall when necessary	Go to the mall every week
Give at least 10% of your income	Only give occasionally
Believe you can be wealthy	Believe you will stay broke
Finding a treasure in every trial	Worrying about everything
Volunteering your time	Not doing for others
Set up boundaries in life	Doing whatever is fun
Having written goals	Having no vision of the future
Communicating with your spouse	Ignoring your spouse's feelings
Being content	Buying new things all the time
Repairing items when broken	Replacing items when broken
Eating out occasionally	Eating out all the time
Paying attention to the small things	Doing without thinking

Most of the ones listed above are bad habits that I had that needed replacing. You may share some of these with me or you may have some that are completely different. But you do have them. I don't say that to be mean, but instead to be realistic. If you are not honest about what is getting in the way of you becoming wealthy and financially free, you will never get where you want to be.

SUMMING UP WEEK 20

This week we are revisiting the subject of bad habits and good ones. There have been several subjects in this book that we have dealt with for 2 weeks instead of one and that is because they are the essential keys to wealth building. Your habits – your actions and your thinking – is one of those subjects.

First, make sure that you keep your list of bad habits that you wanted to replace from the first month all the way through your wealth journey and add to it as necessary. Then, this week, pick the next biggest bad habit that is getting in your way and devise a plan to form a good habit to replace it. A new habit is usually formed within 21 – 30 days with great attention being paid to it. However, even once the new habit is formed, it takes weeks and months to build up your new habit muscles. This is why I didn't readdress this subject until this week. I would recommend, going forward in your wealth journey, that you choose a new habit to form every 3-4 months. This gives you time to make sure you are strong enough with one habit to take a new one on. And if an old bad habit slips in occasionally, and it probably will, don't be discouraged. Stay strong and keep building those money muscles. On to week 21!

WEEK 21

THE CLEANSE

We only have six weeks to go – six weeks until you will have what you need to be wealthy and financially free. Up until now, the things we have learned and done have been mostly big things – steps taken right out of the wealthy people playbook. These last six weeks are going to seem smaller and less important, but they are not. Wealthy people not only focus on the big things in life, but on the small things as well.

One of the fads going around right now is cleansing programs for the body. These programs are designed to cleanse your system of toxins and other bad things that build up over time. This week we are going to go through our own little cleansing program – cleansing our stuff.

The amount of stuff you own and how you take care of that stuff say a lot about what is going on in your life. I walk into many homes and can tell right away one of the main reasons they are having financial trouble. How much stuff you have and how you take care of it is a great indicator as to how you handle your finances. It can also be a great indicator as to how confident you feel about yourself and your life.

YOU AND YOUR STUFF

It is possible that you do not have a lot of stuff sitting around in your home. But all of us have things that we do not use or no longer need. We know that this is a common situation because almost every talk show and every magazine has a professional contributor on this very subject. People tend to think that they can't purge their stuff or organize their home because they weren't born that way. But the truth is anyone can do it if they set their mind to it.

One of the easiest ways is to start small. If you look at your entire house or even a closet that is spilling over, you may become overwhelmed and, therefore, unmotivated to go through it. Anything that seems overwhelming to you can be done by simply breaking it down into small steps. Have you ever walked into your kitchen after a big meal or a party and been so overwhelmed by the mess that you weren't sure where to start? And perhaps you even delayed cleaning up because it seemed like too much. This always happens to me at Christmas when our entire family is here. I have learned, however, how to break this overwhelming task into smaller steps that allow me to conquer the mess and spend time with my family.

The same process can be used on a closet, a drawer or anything that you need to clean or sort through. You may look at your closets and think there is no way I can clean that out – it is just too much. But you can. You just need to take it one step at a time.

Another problem you may come across as you begin your cleansing process is deciding what to get rid of and what to keep. For many people, this is easy, but for just as many, it is a hard decision to make. The best guidelines you can use when trying to decide what to keep and what to get rid of are to be honest about how often you use or wear the item, how long since you have used or worn the item, and when will you use it or wear it again.

This week and this process aren't just about getting rid of all of your stuff. It is okay to have stuff. However it is about getting rid of items that you aren't using anymore and organizing the items that you choose to keep. This process will also help you when it comes to contentment and being content with what you already have which you know is a huge key to wealth. You would be hard pressed to go into a wealthy person's home and find a mess or a lot of stuff just sitting around not being used. This is because wealthy people only buy the things that they really want and will actually use. And they also take care of what they have so that it will last them for a very long time.

CLEAN HOUSE

This used to be one of my favorite television shows. It was a great motivator for me during my cleansing process many years ago. I had actually stopped buying stuff, but I hadn't taken the time to purge my stuff and cleanse myself of items that I no longer used. The show "Clean House" covered two issues: lots of stuff and cleanliness. And the two issues many times go hand in hand. Lucky for me, I only had one of the issues (lots of stuff), but many people have both issues.

We have talked about how to deal with purging your stuff and getting rid of anything that you don't use anymore. And now I want to talk about a clean house. You may think that how clean your house is has nothing to do with your money, but it does. How clean your house is reflects your confidence and how you feel about yourself. When you are confident and happy and have a positive outlook on life, you care about keeping your home and your stuff clean and organized. However, when you are depressed, stressed out and have a negative outlook on life, you don't care much about anything including your home and your stuff.

I have a dear friend who struggled with this problem for years. She had gained weight and in turn she had lost her confidence and her self-esteem was very low. Over time this brought on problems in her marriage as well as in her career. She had lost her job and had no motivation to get another one even though she needed one. And on top of everything else, her house was constantly messy as well as unclean. All of these problems and negative things in her life were a direct result of the lack of confidence she had in herself and in her life, including the dirty, unorganized house. Being a confident person and believing in yourself is a characteristic of the wealthy. If you don't believe you can do anything you set your mind to or dream of doing, you won't do it. No matter what your financial status, being confident and respecting what you have by taking care of it should be a way of life. Don't allow yourself to get so overtaken by the negative that it ends up overshadowing the positive in your life. You are an awesome person. You can do anything that you want to do. But you have to believe it in order to make it happen.

SUMMING UP WEEK 21

This week is all about cleansing and purging your stuff. You will be amazed at how freeing you will feel after you have gotten rid of items that you no longer need or use and organize and clean what you do decide to keep. Doing this may take more than a week, but I want you to start somewhere this week. As you are going through everything, make 4 piles: a keep pile, a donate pile, a sell pile and a trash pile. Sell what you can, donate things that don't have a lot of value and throw away items that are old or broken. Sell anything of value on eBay or Craigslist, have a huge yard sale and donate what doesn't sell. Then take the money and pay off debt with it or put it in your emergency fund. Take everything from the keep pile and give it a home. If you can't find a home for it, then you don't need it.

Along with organizing and purging your stuff, make sure that you are respecting where you live by keeping it clean. This will be easier once you complete the cleansing process because everything will have a home and you won't be fighting the stuff while you are trying to clean. If you need to, make a cleaning schedule and make sure to get your kids involved.

The main differences in wealthy people and in broke people are the way that they think and how they look at things. Wealthy people never have an overabundance. You will find that most of them have a place for everything that they own and they respect and take care of what they do have. Take time this week to begin the cleansing process and use this process to help you in your journey to wealth and financial freedom. On to week 22!

WEEK 22

COMMUNICATING SUCCESSFULLY

It could be said that women are better at communicating than men. But in my many years here on this earth, having been married twice, currently running a successful business, I can tell you that communication is vitally important whether you are a male or a female. I can also tell you that your tone and your body language communicate more to others than your words ever could.

I know that emails and texting are the new way that everyone communicates and I see the plus side of this technology. But I also see the down side. A lot can be lost without the face to face that these communications leave out. I was reading an email recently that had me reading it twice. The tone of the email was one of arrogance and speaking down to the recipient. Knowing the person who wrote it, I can assume that this is not the message that he intended; however, it was the message that was delivered.

There are several close people in my life that I can tell you exactly how they feel about something without them ever having to say a word. This comes across loud and clear in their tone and in their body language. I used to have a bad habit of huffing all of the time. I started doing it as a release for frustration, but then I began to do it every time I didn't get my way or I disagreed with someone. It was never a secret if I didn't agree with you. But this is something that I have worked on over the years and it has gotten better.

Communication is more than just words. And how you communicate with others, especially those close to you, can determine your success in every area of your life including your money. Let's take a look at a few examples so that you can see what I mean.

MARRIAGE

How you communicate with your spouse is, I believe, one of the most important keys to your success, not only in your marriage, but in life. Your spouse is the person that you love most in the world. They are the person that you decided to spend your entire life with.

You would never hurt them on purpose. So why do we? One reason is we are selfish at times. We want to get our way so bad that we forget about the other person. Another reason is communication – what we say and how we say it. Many of us choose to say nothing and some of us choose to say a lot. And when we are upset or passionate about something, we tend to get loud or defensive. I think sometimes we honestly forget who we are talking to. But there are ways to communicate without getting loud or defensive. If you find yourself getting that way, step back and remember who you are talking to and try to find a way to communicate with love and respect, not anger and bitterness.

And always remember that your spouse cannot read your mind. Even if something seems obvious to you, it may not be to them. By the same token, don't try to read their minds. Don't assume that you know what they are thinking or how they will react. Give them a chance to think or react to each situation individually.

Communication in your marriage is vital and will determine your financial success. No matter how much money you make, if you don't communicate with your spouse about how you should handle it and your goals and dreams for the future, you won't keep it. As we have seen already, wealthy people have very successful relationships with their spouses. No matter what your relationship is today, you can start today to make it what you want it to be. Take the first step and keep taking them no matter how the other person treats you. Lead by example and remember if you make your spouse happy, they will want to make you happy.

KIDS

What we teach our kids is crucial. There are two main things to know when it comes to our kids: they watch and learn from you at all times and we are raising adults. This makes communication with and around your kids very important. Kids learn from the ones around them and they become what they are allowed to become. I have seen many parents wonder why their kids are so defiant in the same breath that they are yelling at their spouse. All marriages have disagreements, but how you handle them and the tone in which you handle them are important not only to your marriage, but to your kids.

Just like our spouses, we love our kids very much, but when we are frustrated or angry, we tend to forget that. Make sure that you communicate with your kids - let them know why a rule is a rule, let them know why you made the decision you did, apologize when you make a mistake, let them know why you are concerned about something. Don't just bark orders at them and yell at them. Teach them so that they can learn and understand. One of the greatest experiences of my life is my relationship with my daughter. We talk all of the time, very openly about everything. I let her know where I am coming from and why I made the decision I did. And when it is appropriate, I share my mistakes so that she can learn from them and not repeat them.

Communicate with your kids and help mold them into the adults that they are becoming from day one. Having a great relationship with your kids will help you to win in all areas of your life including your money.

PEOPLE

No one person is better than anyone else. This is a true statement, but do you believe it? When I first went into business, I learned a great thing from the

Cathy family, owners of Chick-fil-A. Whenever you eat at one of their restaurants, they always greet you with "how may I serve you today?" That one word, serve, was the key to my success. It helped me know that the people that I help everyday are important and I am here to serve them the best way that I can.

When you have a serving attitude toward other people, whether it is on your job or in your business or volunteering in the community, you will always have success. Wealthy people serve others and it stems from the Golden Rule – do unto others as you would have them do unto you. Do you like it when someone mistreats you? Do you like it when someone has a bad attitude toward you? Then why is it okay for you to mistreat or have a bad attitude toward other people.

Remembering the Golden Rule will help you tremendously in your wealth journey. Put others first and the money will come along as a result. Treat your boss with respect and you will move up. Treat your customers with a serving attitude and you will make sales. Treat a stranger with dignity and respect and you never know whose life you may change. No one is better than anyone else.

SUMMING UP WEEK 22

Communication is an important part of our lives. And without it, problems can arise. We need to be aware of not only our words, but our tone and our body language. Most of us don't set out to hurt people especially the people who we love the most, but many times lack of communication, bad tone, and some body language can do just that. Take time this week to look at your relationships with your spouse, with your kids, and with other people, friends and strangers alike, and be honest about your communication skills.

Wealthy people tend to be great communicators. They have a way of letting people know where they stand and what they expect without offending them in the process. They have learned how important communication is in everyday life and success and they have worked on their communication skills so that they can speak without offense. You can change how you communicate with your spouse, with your kids and with other people no matter how these people communicate with you. Always remember, you are responsible for you and only you. Do what you know to do and stop worrying about the rest. Be the example that people need to see. On to week 23!

WEEK 23

CONTINUING EDUCATION

Learning shouldn't stop the day you graduate. When I say "continuing education", I don't mean just college. I mean education that continues throughout your entire life. Knowledge is power. You should always want to learn more and become more knowledgeable about things. The more you know about something, the more you can understand it and the better decisions you can make when necessary.

There are many ways to gain this knowledge without ever stepping foot into a classroom and with the internet, that has never been more possible than it is right now. Let's look at a few ways that you can increase your knowledge as you work your way through this thing we call life.

READING

You are increasing your knowledge right now by reading this book. You are learning what wealthy people do to gain their wealth and keep it. And you decided to read this book in hopes that you would learn something new and something that would help you to improve your financial situation.

That is what reading does, whether it is non-fiction or fiction. It expands the mind and helps you to gain knowledge that might change your life. It also gives you different perspectives to consider. Reading can help open up your mind and remove some of the blinders that many of us get over time. I read an autobiography a few years back about a man that, based on what I saw and heard, I didn't care for very much. But what I found out by reading his book was that there was so much more to him than the media showed. And I learned a lot about his position and how difficult his job really was. He took the blame for many things just because of the position that he was in, but he struggled very hard to make the decisions that he felt were right.

If I had been closed minded or only believed what I saw, I wouldn't have gained an understanding of the person even though I didn't always agree with him. That is one of the great things that reading can do for you.

One of my personal growth goals is to read at least one non-fiction and one fiction book per month. This goal has never changed over the years. Sometimes I exceed the goal, but reading is something that I never want to remove from my life. I learn too much from it. There are no limitations on the subjects that I read as well. I read anything from a book about wealth building to a book about Linda Ronstadt. I read anything from a book about how to break a bad habit to a book about how to be a better leader. I never limit the areas in which I want to gain knowledge.

Reading is essential to personal growth and to wealth building. When you expand your mind, you are better equipped to make decisions in your life and your money. And those better decisions will carry you to a life of wealth and financial freedom.

HOBBIES

Hobbies are a great thing to have. And it is even better to have more than one hobby. I know many wealthy people who learn a new hobby every year. Hobbies are simply something fun that you enjoy doing. Hobbies can range in cost from free to extremely expensive, so you may be limited there, but hobbies are another great way to expand your mind.

Hobbies can also be very relaxing. We need to take time out every day for ourselves. Whether it is quiet time in the morning, a walk around the block at lunch or a spa treatment every few months, we need to pamper ourselves.

Expand your knowledge using hobbies. Hobbies are not only fun, but also a great way to learn a new skill as well as new information that can move you forward in your journey.

EDUCATION

Education doesn't always have to be obtained on a college campus. And you don't have to go broke to obtain an education. Education is defined as the knowledge resulting from a learning process. So anything you do that results in new knowledge is education.

A great way to obtain knowledge through education is to take a class. You don't have to get a degree in what you want to learn; you can just take a class. Classes can be taken at a local community center or tech school or you can take individual classes at a community college or university without pursuing a degree.

Learn something new every year whether it is a skill, a concept or just information. Even if you have an accountant, take an accounting class so you have knowledge in this area. Even though you have a financial adviser, take a mutual fund class so you have knowledge in that area. Take a class in psychology just to see how the brain works. Take a class in computers just to see how they work. Knowledge is power and the more you know, the better off you will be. According to G.I. Joe, "knowing is half the battle", so gain knowledge wherever you can. Education leads to knowledge. Knowledge leads to better decisions. And better decisions lead to wealth and financial freedom.

SUMMING UP WEEK 23

Wealthy people are always learning something new. They never sit back and let everyone tell them what to do and they just do it. They are constantly educating themselves through reading, having and learning new hobbies, and taking classes that interest them and increase their knowledge. Never give up on your education. Keep expanding your mind, your skills and your knowledge until the day that you die. I can't say it enough – Knowledge is power! On to week 24!

10 Non-Fiction Books to Get You Started

"Making Good Habits, Breaking Bad Ones" by Joyce Meyer

"Thou Shalt Prosper" by Rabbi Daniel Lapin

"Love and Respect" by Dr. Emerson Eggerichs

"The Millionaire Mind" by Dr. Thomas Stanley

"The Millionaire Next Door" by Dr. Thomas Stanley

"48 Days to the Work You Love" by Dan Miller

"How Rich People Think" by Steve Siebold

"The Total Money Makeover" by Dave Ramsey

The Bible

"The ABC's of Personal Finance" by Debbi King

WEEK 24

ALL ABOUT YOU

Earlier I talked about how being selfish will not bring you the wealth and financial freedom that you want. We are going to make an exception for this one week and this one week only. This doesn't mean everything will go your way this week or that you will get everything that you want. What it does mean is that you are going to take the week to learn all about you.

We tend to know much more about other people than we know about ourselves. We also know more about ourselves than we are usually willing to admit. You can never get to where you need to be if you can't face who you are and where you are. You are an awesome person, but you, like all of us, have things about you that you don't like and that get in the way of your goals and dreams. This week, I want you to be completely honest with yourself about those things are holding you back and begin to do what you need to do to be who you want to be.

OUR EXCUSE BAG

We all have an excuse bag. For some it is a tote and for some it is a whole set of luggage. But we all have one. Why do you think you are not wealthy yet? Do you think it is because of how you were raised? Do you think that it is because you have an awful boss? Do you think that it is because the banks are just corporate sharks? This may all be true, but these are just excuses. Every one of these things, and every other excuse you have, is just that – an excuse. An excuse is simply you trying to remove blame from yourself and put it on something or someone else.

After I filed for bankruptcy 17 years ago, I continued to handle my finances the same way. A lot of it was habit, which we have covered in great detail, but a large part of it was also my excuses and my lack of taking responsibility. You see, as long as I kept excusing my behavior and blamed everyone else, nothing was going to change. It wasn't until I threw out my excuse bag, owned my mistakes, learned from them and changed my actions and thinking that I began to win in the area of money (and life).

I know that one of the hardest things to do is to realize that you messed up, made a bad decision, or made a mistake. And it takes a really strong person to admit a mistake, learn from it and make it better. You are a strong person; therefore, you can do this. I can't even put into words how freeing this process can be once you begin to take responsibility and how much it will change your life.

You see, when you keep making excuses and blaming other people, you are limited in your solutions. When it is someone else's fault, you have to wait on them to fix it. But as soon as you realize that you are responsible, you then have the control to be able to fix the problem without waiting on anyone else.

I very rarely will talk politics. But I am always saddened by the way that many people believe that the government is responsible for their problems and it is the government's responsibility to fix them. Why should the government bail you out because you bought a house that you couldn't afford and using a loan that wasn't quite right? Why should the government pay you for years because you can't find that "perfect" job? Now, don't get mad at me. Just think about it for a minute. When you buy a house, you are given a contract and the terms of the loan. You know what you are getting into before you sign and if you don't, you shouldn't sign. Right now there are many jobs to be had and everyone has the ability to start their own business and make double their old income. You can solve your own problems. If you bought a house at a bad deal, own it. And then do what you need to do to fix it. If you lose your job, make it your new full time job to network and find a better job. And if you can't within the six months of unemployment, start your own business and make all the money you want.

Stop playing the blame game. It will never get you where you want to be. If you make a mistake, and we all make them every day, own it, learn from it, and fix it. A mistake is a positive thing if you learn from it. But if you keep making the same ones over and over, there is a bigger problem. Mistakes will not prevent you from being wealthy, but keeping your excuse bag around and playing the blame game will never bring you the wealth and financial freedom that you desire.

YOU ARE AN AUTHOR

Everyone is an author. You may not have any books

published, but you are an author none the less. You are the author of your own story – your life. Many of you have been letting someone else write your story and so far it is not a best seller. In order to be successful, you have to maintain control of your life. You can't let others control you and your decisions.

This also goes back to responsibility. You can change the direction of your story much quicker if you own what mistakes you made, learn from them and change them. Even if you made some of your decisions because of other people, you allowed them to control that and that was not wise. So own it, take back control and write your own story. Remember this – you have to live your life, no one else does. So live the life that you want to live and not the life that others think you should be living.

I was actually talking with my mom this morning about this exact thing. People are judged by whether they live in a house or in an apartment or whether they rent or own. That is just ridiculous. You are no less of a person if you rent than if you buy. You have to do what is best for you. If you can't afford a house right now, there is no shame in that. And if you choose to rent for the rest of your life, there is no shame in that either. Yes, a house is a good investment and one of only several positive investments out there, but it still may not be for everyone. What does it matter where you live as long as you are somewhere that you can afford and you are happy. Other people don't have to pay your bills nor do they have a say in what makes you happy, so don't let their snobby behavior control your decisions.

WHO AM I?

This week is all about you. It is not only about the choices and the decisions, but it is also about you, the person. Do you know who you really are or have you been so busy trying to please everyone that you lost yourself somewhere? That was me. I know many of you do not struggle with this and that is great, but I also know that many of you do, just as I did. Trying to please everyone else and be what everyone else wanted me to be contributed to my debt and my negative financial situation. This is why I believe that many of you struggle with this whether you realize it or not.

Learning who you really are and who you want to be is going to be a process, but a process that is necessary. It is imperative that you stop living for everyone else and live the life that you want to live. And part of doing that is learning who you are, your faults and your good qualities and deciding who you want to be and how to get there.

This week, in addition to getting rid of your excuses and stopping the blame game, make a list of all of your good qualities and your bad ones. Then write out qualities that you would like to have and develop a plan on how to achieve that goal. For example, I had a tendency to want everything done right away and if someone didn't do something right away, I became agitated and impatient. This is not a good quality when you are in a relationship, you have kids, or deal with people in general. It also affected my finances in a negative way because I was quick to make decisions and not take time, even a few minutes to think something through. Once I realized this about myself, I began to work on my patience and I began to realize that not everybody does things as fast as me, and that is okay. I also learned to slow down myself which has helped me tremendously.

Realizing this about myself was hard to face originally, but owning it and changing it was life changing. You are awesome. We all have good and bad traits, but if you can be authentic and genuine and be exactly who you want to be, that is all you will ever need. Don't let anyone tell you who to be and how to act. Be yourself and be more.

SUMMING UP WEEK 24

Don't let what is wrong in your life blind you to all the great things in your life. You are an awesome person. Maybe there are some things about yourself that you wish to change and that is okay. Begin this week to make those changes. Don't do anything or make any decisions based on what other people think. Don't let other people control you. You are the author of your own story and your story has the potential to be a best seller. But only if you take over writing it. Stop blaming other people and stop making excuses – period. If you made a decision or said something that you shouldn't have, own it. If you forgot something, own it. You are a human being who makes mistakes. Make it right, forgive yourself, and move on. Dwelling on the negative – whether it is decisions, actions, or personality traits – will never get you to the wealth and financial freedom you want. Do what you can do, control what you can control, and let the rest alone. On to week 25!

WEEK 25

NEED VS. WANT

"I need an iPhone." "I need another purse." "We need a new house." These are words heard around this country every day. And there is only one thing wrong with these sentences. The word "need" should be replaced with the word "want". With every generation, the wants get larger. Kids today want everything and if you tell them no, you are a horrible parent (according to them). And somewhere in their mind, they believe that they need these things to survive.

One of the main reasons that they believe this is because they truly have no idea what it is to actually need something. They have all of their needs met and they have so many extras that they cannot grasp what it means to really be in need. In one county near me, 70,000 people don't have enough money to feed their families every day. There are adults and children right here in my neighborhood that do not get three meals a day. And in my house, we not only have three meals a day, but we have snacks and sodas for treats and we eat out about once a week. We not only have our needs met, but we have so many of our wants as well. But yet sometimes my daughter gets upset because I won't order a pizza.

This is what she sees out in her world. It is very hard for her to grasp being in need because no matter how bad money problems have gotten over the years, we have always had our needs met. Wealthy people understand the difference between a need and a want. You may be thinking that this is true because they have plenty of money. But actually it is understanding a need versus a want that helped them to reach their wealth status.

You may be wondering what I mean by that. What I am talking about is the law of replacement versus upgrade. Let me ask you a question – do you get the latest device as soon as it comes out even though you already have a perfectly good device? And when you do replace this device, do you sell the old one or do you throw it in a drawer? Let me ask you another question – do you buy new items such as appliances, cars, furniture, etc. just because you want the latest and the greatest or because they no longer work?

Let me insert a caveat here – it is okay to want and buy new things, if you can afford them. That is not the issue or the point of this week. It is about truly recognizing and realizing the difference in a need and a want. Doing this will help you to look at a situation and make a better decision and will also help you move forward in your wealth journey. We are an upgrade society, but to the detriment of our financial future. We need to become more of a replacement society in order to secure our financial future. Wealthy people do upgrade occasionally, but they mostly replace. For example, most wealthy people have flat screen televisions. But most of them did not run right out and buy a flat screen the day it came out. Many of them probably even waited until the last possible moment when their old television wouldn't work with their cable anymore. And I would be willing to bet that their old television was at least 10 years old.

Wealthy people buy better quality and keep things longer than broke people. Broke people want the latest fad now. Wealthy people will keep a couch for 30 years. Wealthy people will own laminate countertops. Wealthy people will use ivory colored appliances. Again, this does not mean that wealthy people never upgrade to granite countertops; many of them do. But they do it only if they want to and they do it when it is right for them financially and not the second it becomes a fad. Wealthy people don't care at all about fads. They buy what they want, what will last them for years and what they can afford.

I always share one of my aha moments to help people understand the point I am trying to make and I hope it will help you as much as it helped me. Years ago, I had a washing machine that stopped working. So my husband and I went washing machine shopping. When I went to Lowe's, I found what I thought was the perfect washing machine – a red front loader (my laundry room is just off of the kitchen where I have red accents everywhere). So of course, this was exactly what I wanted. But the price was more than I had budgeted to spend. Also, my dryer was in great shape so I didn't need a new dryer. After shopping, we decided to go home and talk out our options in order to make the best decision.

After a lot of discussion, I all of the sudden had a big aha moment. First, if I bought the red washing machine, I should buy the red dryer or it would look funny and also I didn't know if they would have the matching dryer available when I needed it. I had the money to buy both, but we had set a budget on just the washing machine and a simple washing machine at that. I realized that I wanted the red washer and dryer because that was what was in style and popular. Also, there were so many bells and whistles on it that I didn't need and having those bells and whistles meant a better chance for something to go wrong in the future. Also, what if we had to move and the color of my laundry room/kitchen changed. And at the time, there was major complaining by consumers of the smell that comes from front loaders due to the buildup. There were too many negatives to ignore even though it was pretty.

At that moment, standing in my kitchen, I realized that I was lucky to even have a washing machine. My grandmother didn't and she survived just fine. All I really needed was a reliable name brand, simple washing machine that would look okay next to my dryer. And I needed to buy it at the best price possible. So that is what I did and I never regretted it once. And I know that if I had purchased the other set, I would have, at times, had some small regret.

This is what realizing the difference in a want and a need is. Decisions like this are what will bring you wealth. Does this mean that if I had bought the set I would never be wealthy or that wealthy people don't own these washer/dryer sets? No, but it does mean that you have to make the right decisions for your finances not only with the present in mind, but also with the future in mind.

Almost everything you have is a want in the sense that you could survive without it. You need a roof over your head, but you don't need a 2000 square foot home. You need food in your belly, but you don't need to eat out. You need a car to drive, but you don't need a new car. You need lights and heat in your house, but you do not need internet or cable. A 2000 square foot home, eating out, a new car and internet and cable are all wants. It is okay to have them, but understand that they are wants not needs.

I will say this again – simply being able to honestly label everything in the correct way – a need or a want – will help you tremendously with your perspective of things. And your perspective is a huge key to your wealth. When you know that something is really a want and not a need, it will help you to be more content and patient and will help you to have a different perspective regarding the decision. This way when and if you choose to buy something, you will have no regrets because you know you were honest with yourself, you thought it through and you made the best decision possible for your wealth journey and your financial freedom.

SUMMING UP WEEK 25

Need versus want is one of the most controversial things that I teach. It is the thing that I catch the most flack for. It is one of the most argued points in any of my sessions or workshops. And it is simply because people believe that I am telling them that they can't have something if it is a want. And that is simply not true. You can have anything that you want. My house is full of wants. This week is about truly discerning the difference in a need and a want. If you believe that something is a need, you will place it as a higher priority than a want. So if you believe that you need a new outfit, even though your closet is overflowing, then you will justify using a credit card or even using your rent money to make that purchase. If you realize that a new outfit is a want, then you will not mortgage your future for it and you will buy it when you can afford it.

My challenge to you is this – this week, go around your house, room by room, and make two different lists – a list of items that you need and a list of items that are luxuries (wants). Again, this is not to make you feel bad. This is to help you realize how blessed you really are and how wealthy you already are. And I want you to be completely honest – 20 pairs of shoes is not a necessity; 2 or 3 pairs are needed, everything else is wanted. To help you with this, think back to how your grandparents lived and realize that they were happy fulfilled people even though they didn't have a microwave.

Once you do this, you will be able to begin to switch your thinking from that of "I'm broke" to that of "I'm very blessed". This change in thinking will help you tremendously in your wealth journey and help you realize the financial freedom that you want to have. On to week 26!

WEEK 26

THE FINALE

Well, here you are! You are on the final week of what I hope has been a great 26 weeks for you. I hope that you have truly taken in the information of each week. You may not be wealthy in your bank account at the end of this week, but you are definitely ready to be wealthy and financially free. If you take seriously every single week and do everything that this book suggests, you will be wealthy and financially free.

Being wealthy is not all about how much money you make. It is about what you do with what you make. A person making $25,000 can become wealthy and a person making $250,000 can be broke. Realizing this will give you the hope and courage you need to become wealthy. The first step in becoming wealthy and financially free is believing that you can. If you have gotten to this week, and you still don't believe that you can be wealthy, you won't be. If you believe that it is all about luck and how you were raised or where you went to college, you will never be wealthy. When my daughter was little and she began to wonder if Santa was real or not, I used to simply tell her "you have to believe to receive". That holds true for adults as well as children. If you don't believe something will happen, then odds are it won't. Or if it does, you won't embrace it for the awesomeness that it is.

You should never become obsessed about being wealthy. If money is all you think about, you will miss out on the greatness of life. And the truth is that you will probably never have enough money. If you had $2 million in the bank, you would want $3 million just to feel secure. The more we have, the more we want. What you need to do is set up your life – your decision making, your actions, your thinking, etc. – in such a way that you can have what you need as well as what you want.

If you have $25,000 in an emergency fund, you are probably wealthier than you were before and now you have the freedom to handle an emergency if it comes up – up to $25,000. But you don't yet have the freedom to handle a $30,000 emergency. That is why wealth is more of a state of being than a dollar amount. Sam Walton became a billionaire and still drove around in a used old pickup truck. He knew that being wealthy wasn't a social status. It was a way of living.

I would be willing to bet that if you looked around at everything that you own and added up everything that it cost you, you would realize how wealthy you have the potential to be. And this doesn't include all of the money you spent on one time gratification. Now, again, these things are not wrong and having those things is not wrong. But you may not be as broke as you think. Odds are you do not have an income problem, but instead you have a lifestyle problem.

Here is a good thing to remember – money can come and money can go. I know people who have become wealthy, lost it all and rebuilt themselves again because they had a wealthy attitude. But I also know people who have become wealthy, lost it all, and stayed broke for the rest of their lives. This happens a lot when wealth comes too quickly or is handed to you. But it can happen even if you have built your wealth from the ground up because it can be tempting to make a shift in your thinking the more money you make.

Being humble is a great characteristic of a truly wealthy person. This is when you realize how blessed you are and that money and things are only a part of your world, not your whole world. Most truly wealthy people don't flaunt their wealth and if you asked them if they would consider themselves wealthy, most would say no. There are many fake wealthy people out there, but they are easier to spot because they want you to know that they are wealthy. To them, status is everything.

This book and this process has been about taking steps and changing things in order to set yourself up to be wealthy and financially free. If you have done everything in this book, you will begin to see wealth almost immediately. Remember, we talked about in the introduction how wealth has a different definition to different people. When I first had an emergency fund of $2500, I felt wealthy and that gave me the courage to keep making positive decisions and to keep building my wealth. I began to think more and more like a person of wealth and this has brought positive changes in my life.

Does this mean that I can sit back and coast now? Not at all. I will spend the rest of my life doing everything in this book because I know that it will bring the best financial results possible. And if for any reason, everything was taken from me and I had to start over, I know that I have the ability to build my wealth up again because it has become my lifestyle, not my diet.

As I conclude this book, I just want to tell you that I know that no matter where you are right now financially, you can become wealthy and financially free. I know this because I hit the bottom 18 years ago and I have spent the last 18 years studying and learning how to build wealth and how to respect the money that I have been blessed with. I learned that if I couldn't handle and respect a small amount, how would I ever handle a large amount. So I worked on handling what I had so that I would be prepared when there was more.

I encourage you today to believe enough in yourself to know that you are in control of your future – no one else. You can be anything that you want to be and have anything that you want to have. To do this, you may have to make some changes, maybe even some big, hard changes. But it is definitely worth it. Be more and enjoy every day of your journey to wealth and financial freedom. God bless you!

www.ingramcontent.com/pod-product-compliance
Lightning Source LLC
Chambersburg PA
CBHW051211170526
45166CB00005B/1849